HOW TO BEAT
WALL STREET

JB MARWOOD

First published by The New Minimalist in 2013

Cover and book design by The New Minimalist 2013

www.thenewminimalist.com

Proofreading and editing by Copy Correct

www.copycorrect.ca

ISBN 978-1494228170

Copies are available at special rates for bulk orders.
Further copies are available from
www.jbmarwood.com

DISCLAIMER

THE LIFE YOU CAN SAVE

10% of royalties are donated to charities recommended by the life you can save project, a movement of people fighting extreme poverty—http://www.thelifeyoucansave.org

SYSTEM CODE & EXTRAS

Please note that trading system code, Excel spreadsheets and bonus extras come free with the download pack that accompanies this book. To obtain a copy visit jbmarwood.com

CONTENTS

CHAPTER 1:
TRADING FUNDAMENTALS

CHAPTER 2:
TIMING

CHAPTER 3:
RISK

CHAPTER 4:
TRADING TIPS

CHAPTER 5:
TECHNICAL ANALYSIS

CHAPTER 6:
TRADING SYSTEMS

CHAPTER 7:
RESOURCES AND BONUS MATERIAL

FOREWORD

Following the financial crisis of 2007-2008, many veteran traders were faced with a totally different financial landscape in which to operate. The 'new normal,' a term first coined by Pimco trader Mohammed El-Erian, became the finance community's go-to phrase for a world order which bore more similarities with the post-Depression era than anything investors had previously experienced.

This 'new normal,' characterized by persistently sluggish growth, high unemployment and political wrangling over debt ceilings and budget deficits, is now five years on and shows no sign of abating.

But it is not only political parties that stand to lose from the new period of economic stagnation. Financial markets, as a result of huge injections of artificial liquidity from central banks, now reside atop a mountain of debt and are precariously placed, should we see any reduction in liquidity or future drop in growth.

Indeed, it could be argued that the super loose monetary policy used in response to the biggest recession since the 1930s has actually heightened risk, and the resulting artificial rally in global stock markets has created a world in which markets are now scarily dependent on the money flows from central banks.

Much like a heroin addict becomes dependent upon the drug, the financial markets have become dependent on the monthly injections of quantitative easing from the Federal Reserve, and it is for this reason that every Federal Open Market Committee meeting is now watched with bated breath by most traders.

Just like the symptoms of withdrawal when such a drug is taken away, the potential for significant market volatility is profound. Given that these risks are so prevalent, there has never been a more crucial time to learn about the financial markets.

Inflation onslaught

At the heart of the problem that financial markets face is a battle between stagnant economic growth and the coming onslaught of inflation, brought on by years of easy money.

Normally, this would not present too much of a problem since periods of economic stagnation can be reinvigorated by central bank intervention.

However, to believe this is to forget that central banks have now used up all of their bullets. Indeed, central banks now sit on a mountain of debt with no alternative but to scale back, or 'taper,' as the Federal Reserve like to call it – language that has already caused significant turmoil in stock markets over recent months.

With the prospect of future monetary unwinding, the already fragile growth picture seen in most developed nations has the potential to stall even further.

Indeed, recessions typically occur every 4 to 6 years in developed countries, meaning we are now overdue.

Financial deficits need austerity, not additional debt; which is why when the next slowdown comes, as it surely will, the financial comedown is likely to be as severe (if not worse than that of 2007-2008).

Central banks cannot inject any more liquidity because the debt is too high and they cannot cut interest rates because rates are already at zero.

You can see now why the propping up of huge, failed institutions is rarely conducive to a smooth running financial system.

So what will be the future of finance and how will the next billionaire traders make their fortunes? One answer lies in the new breed of technology. If history has taught us anything it is that those who succeed are generally those who are able to embrace new frontiers.

The new frontiers

It is true that the Internet has brought with it many advantages and benefits to traders. However, the world we live in is now faced with information overload and a rapidly changing business environment.

For financial markets, this means new risks – long tail events and flash crashes, as well as, new opportunities such as social trading and new analytics. (You will find these subjects addressed later in the book.)

Traversing the new world, with its gluttony of information, requires ever more sophisticated tools to analyze data, discover new metrics and respond to them in a timely manner. However, just as information needs filtering, markets need overseeing, and as central banks begin to unwind, the 'new normal' may well give way to a new type of order.

Stagflation, a combination of stagnation and inflation, is one possibility. Where there is sluggish growth but strong inflation, prompting a world where real assets become the best protectors of value. A world where rises in asset prices give the general populace the illusion of wealth but not the real thing.

In truth, no one knows what this world order may look like but if we have learned anything over the last few hundred years it is that while markets may change, the people who trade them rarely do. The fundamental skills needed to profit from the markets therefore are likely to stay much the same.

Combining them with the new breed of technology could become a winning formula for the next decade.

With such risk and opportunity looming, there has never been a better time to educate yourself about the way financial markets operate.

MY STORY

It's fair to say that Monday, September 15, 2008, was a pretty eventful day for me. Not only was it the day that Lehman Brothers declared bankruptcy after a weekend fraught with rumour but it was my first day in a new job as a futures trader in the City of London, England.

Six months of intense training and three months of live demo trading, alongside two other recent graduates, had all boiled down to this and we were eager to go.

We came in on that Monday morning to find that US stock markets were already down nearly 200 points before the market had even opened. We had heard the rumours about Lehman Brothers over the weekend but this was practically unheard of. We could only sit and watch as the market went on to decline further throughout the day, posting its biggest drop since 9/11.

By Wednesday, markets were reeling and the Dow Jones Industrial Average ended the day down by 500 points (over 4%). It was a pattern that was to be repeated frequently over the next few months as the credit crunch caused a perfect storm of events culminating in the Dow's largest ever one-day loss of more than 1,000 points and several months of severe volatility.

Back in the trading room, things were manic and even veteran traders had not seen anything like it before. We spent those first couple of days just watching, too scared to place a trade. At first, we couldn't believe our bad fortune that we had managed to start our trading careers during some of the toughest conditions in the last 100 years. However, looking back, it was probably the best thing that could have happened.

Although it was tough, surviving the crisis meant learning everything at breakneck speed and it has made me an infinitely better trader today.

It's for that reason I have put together this book containing all the knowledge and secrets I have learned over the last five years. I have consumed hundreds of books and articles and put in thousands of hours of trading; everything I have learned has been put into this book.

It's not supposed to be a trading bible, far from it. We will never stop learning in this business. But it does provide information that should be useful to beginners as well as more advanced traders.

There is a hell of a lot of information out there in the world, some good, but most of it bad, which is why I have kept everything in the book short and snappy, so you don't have to waste time getting to the good stuff. In fact, I have set it out almost like a series of blog posts so you can flick through to the bits that you're interested in, if you want. At the end of the book you'll also find a resources section which you can use to read up further on the topics addressed here.

I hope by passing on this knowledge, you are able to become a smarter, more informed trader.

All the best with beating the markets.

HOW IT ALL BEGAN

Trading is a fact of life and has been around since the beginning of civilization. In fact, the first futures exchange can be traced back to Ancient Greece where the Greek philosopher Thales developed a way of predicting olive harvests.

Thales was able to predict when a good harvest was around the corner and made agreements with local olive growers at fixed prices, depositing money with them in order to take advantage of the harvest when it came around.

The olive growers were happy to agree to the transaction since they did not know what the harvest would be like and were effectively hedging their future income in case of a poor harvest.

When the time came, the harvest was indeed excellent and Thales was able to sell back his stake for a substantial profit. Thus, the first futures contract was settled.

Today, the rules are a bit clearer and a futures contract is defined as a contract between two parties to buy or sell something at an agreed price today, with the delivery and payment occurring at a later date.

Futures thus provide risk insurance to producers and holders at a relatively low cost and are the perfect vehicles for trading.

Some products such as forex (foreign exchange market) can be traded on spot markets, but for all intents and purposes there is very little difference between the two. The only real difference is that futures products are settled at some time in the future, whereas spot products are settled daily. Whether you use futures or spot markets, the principles for trading them are the same.

Trading vs. investing

Throughout this book, we cover some aspects of trading and some of investing but in both we mainly deal with stocks, bonds, commodities, forex and ETFs (exchange-traded funds) – any product that lends itself to be freely traded on a central exchange.

For further clarification, we denote trading to be anytime that something is bought with the intention of selling it at a later date for a profit. Anything else shall be deemed as investing.

Getting started

A trader is someone who buys and sells goods, currencies or stocks and makes money by buying something at a low price and selling it a higher price, after taking into account the cost of commissions.

It's important to understand this and not get side-tracked as everything boils down to this one simple truth.

Anyone can become a successful trader if they put in the hours and these days there are plenty of ways to get started. All you need is a computer, an Internet connection and a bit of money. If you have those you can connect to a broker and be trading cotton futures, soybeans, gold futures, silver or Nasdaq stocks in a matter of seconds.

Becoming successful, however, is a different matter, and the game of trading has an immensely steep learning curve.

I can think of no other career quite like trading, where the risks are so great yet the opportunities are so vast. For an exceptional trader, there really is no limit to the amount of money that can be made.

In the end, it really doesn't matter who you are or where you come from. In the eyes of the markets', everyone is equal and if you put in the required effort you can succeed. Not everyone will of course; it is suggested that between 60-90% of retail traders will lose overall.

The majority of those are amateurs, gamblers who play the markets for excitement or out of curiosity. It is actually a very small group of traders who are responsible for 90% of profits in the markets. They are disciplined professionals and have worked hard to hone their craft over many years.

So you could be either one of those who wants to get rich quick, who plays the markets out of boredom and who wants to find the shortcuts to riches but never finds them. Or, you could be a disciplined professional, committed to becoming the best trader you can be.

I know which I would rather be.

Contained in this book are some of the secrets used by the small minority of traders that manage to win, time and time again.

But first we need to start at the beginning.

CHAPTER 1:
TRADING FUNDAMENTALS

TRADING PHILOSOPHIES

There are thousands, if not millions, of traders in the world and nearly all of them have their own unique strategy to profit from the markets. Some use technical indicators, some fundamental data and others look at news releases.

There are, however, two very broad philosophies that I believe most traders ascribe to: mean reversion or trend following.

Mean reversion

Mean reversion traders typically believe that market prices fluctuate around a certain level of equilibrium, be it the recent mean or something else like intrinsic value.

They therefore believe that when a security deviates from this level, it is an opportunity to make a trade in the opposite direction and profit when the price returns to equilibrium.

Since markets trade in ranges most of the time, mean reversion is a very popular method of trading the markets – particularly among day traders – where big trends tend to be less pronounced and there is more 'noise' in the markets.

It all depends on your own world view and how you see markets operating. If you believe mean reversion is true, there are plenty of ways to approach the markets (which we look at later in this book).

Trend following

'The trend is your friend, until the end when it bends.'

This is a common saying among traders who believe in the other trading philosophy of trend following. Trend following basically describes the simple belief that markets move in trends.

In other words, the belief that if market prices move in one direction for long enough it is possible to trade in the direction of that movement and make a profit.

Trend following is thus the polar opposite of mean reversion and many trend followers trade trends irrespective of fundamental events or news flow.

It is often said that markets range approximately 60% of the time and trend the rest. So trend followers may often encounter more losing trades than other traders, but this is generally compensated by bigger moves and therefore bigger wins. A win ratio of just 40% can be considered a good win ratio for trend followers.

Once again, we refer to trend following throughout this book and give many ways of putting this philosophy into practice.

Different opinions

As you may have noticed, these two philosophies are broad and many traders do not fit into either of these two categories definitively.

I am a fan of trend following strategies and prefer to use these in most of my trading. However, I also believe that mean reversion can work well and know many traders who take this approach.

Instead of worrying about which strategies work the best, it is more important to find out what works for you and what style suits your personality. Only by doing so will you be able to trade in a relaxed and confident way.

One thing I have certainly learned over the years is that there is more than one way for a trader to make a living from the market. Traders can hedge, speculate or make short-term bets and that's why traders can take several different forms.

DIFFERENT TYPES OF TRADERS

Quants

Starting with the fastest traders of all, quants are the high frequency traders who trade using quantitative methods and with complex computer algorithms. They are sometimes given a bad name in the industry, after being blamed for the 1987 crash, but quants tend to be technically savvy individuals who are able to harness automated algorithms to find minute inefficiencies in the market.

Becoming a quant might be difficult, because to succeed quants need super fast connections (such as fibre optic lines straight to the exchange) and expensive computers. This is why they often work for big institutions such as the major banks. Their trades are often so fast, operating between the bid and the ask price, that they are not even noticed by the rest of the markets.

Scalpers

One up from the quants, scalpers also operate in the short-term, but they may do so manually or by using a computer program.

Scalpers look to profit from inefficiencies in markets and can hold trades for anything from a couple of seconds to a couple of hours. Scalpers have been in the markets since the beginning with the idea being that markets are forever fluctuating around.

Scalpers use this fact to profit from the 'noise' so that when a market spikes up or down, they will quickly enter and hope to pull one or two pips from a quick reversal. To be a scalper takes a lot of skill and practice and usually a lot of discipline but it can certainly be an interesting way to trade. Both scalpers and quants are very useful to financial markets since they enter lots of trades and provide liquidity to the markets.

Day traders (or technical traders)

Day traders enter and close their trades on a daily basis, rarely holding any positions overnight. Typically, they trade off charts using technical indicators such as pivot points or moving average lines to justify their trades.

They may also take into account fundamental factors and news releases – perhaps buying or selling a stock the moment an economic figure is released. Some day traders may also use strategies to hedge their trades as they go.

Swing traders

Swing traders typically hold positions for a couple of days, but not normally weeks. They are therefore less active than day traders but they do trade frequently enough to have to stay tuned to the markets at all times. They may use technical indicators such as trend lines or resistance channels to identify profit but are just as likely to look at fundamental news flow. They also look out for the possibility of reactions to upcoming news releases and events.

Position traders

Position traders take much longer-term positions and hold positions for weeks, months or years. They are therefore just slightly down from buy and hold investors in terms of time frames. Position traders study big macroeconomic trends in order to find the long-term moves that can often define a market for years. They are also likely to enter big short-position trades and use hedging strategies to build a successful and stable portfolio.

All of the above

It is also possible to be one, none, or many of these different trading styles combined. Some traders concentrate on one market and one style only, perfecting their technique as much as they can, while others take a bit of each style depending upon the situation. For example, a trader might take long-term positions but keep a little bit of capital in reserve, in order to profit from short-term opportunities when they arrive.

In general, the shorter the time frame you trade, the harder it is for you to make a profit. That's just one of the facts of life, so make sure to think carefully about what kind of trader you want to become.

A closer look at position trading

There are many options when it comes to trading the markets but position trading is one type that often steals the headlines. The main reason for this is that position trading allows longer-term positions to be built up over time and therefore facilitates some of the biggest profits.

In fact, some of the most famous traders in the world and biggest hedge funds can be described as position traders. George Soros, Warren Buffett, John Paulson – they are all famous for taking big, long-term positions according to their views on markets.

To sum up then, position trading is any trading style where trades are held open for a long period of time. Some may argue that any trade that is held for longer than a day constitutes position trading but it is generally accepted that position trading relates to trades being held for weeks, months or years.

Another view, is that position trading describes any trade that is placed according to fundamental analysis on the market and only closed once those fundamentals change. Although this is not always the case with position traders, it is certainly true that the majority of position traders use fundamental analysis to enter the markets.

Fundamental analysis

Fundamental analysis is best described as any analysis that looks at data relating to economics or the big picture numbers that operate behind the market. It is therefore not directly interested in the price and can also include top down or bottom up analysis.

As fundamental analysts, position traders study the market rigorously in order to find the big macroeconomic trends that enable them to make huge multi-month or multi-year profits. They study such factors as unemployment, GDP (gross domestic product), retail sales or the outlook for interest rates and they have a firm grasp of how global markets interact with each other.

Because of this, many position traders spend large amounts of time on the sidelines, often putting their money into cash or treasury bills (T-Bills) and waiting for the next big opportunity to emerge.

While some traders such as Warren Buffett waste no time in entering their full position when the opportunity comes, others, such as George Soros, prefer to drip their money into markets gradually, testing their hypothesis and targeting the best possible entry price.

Because of this long-term-ism position traders need a totally different approach to risk tolerance than short-term traders. While short-term traders place very tight stops in the markets to reduce their risk of losing money, this is a flawed strategy for position traders, since they are unconcerned about the minor fluctuations in the markets.

Rather, position traders look for the big trends and need to have a very strong tolerance for losses in order to be able to ride them out over time. In this way, they often need to keep trades relatively small at first, building them up as they progress, and they need to be supremely confident about their trades in order to not get dissuaded when the position is losing money.

Some people like to argue that there is more money to be made trading the markets in the short-term, but it is hard to argue against the effectiveness of position trading considering some of the most successful traders in the world are position traders. George Soros, Warren Buffett and Jim Rogers are just three good examples.

Famous position traders

George Soros

Born in Hungary in 1930, George Soros is one of the most famous position traders of all time, not least for his role in 'Black Wednesday' when he was dubbed the man who 'broke the Bank of England' and netted $1bn in profits from a short position in the British pound.

Since then, Soros has continued to beat the market over several decades, through a combination or rigorous fundamental analysis and gut instinct. He is often said to close trades when he starts to feel backache, an indication that something is not right. He also takes the view which he calls 'reflexivity,' – that the movements in markets can actually affect fundamental conditions just as much as the other way around. Soros has written about this theory in a number of books. (Several of which are included in the Resources and links section at the end of this book.)

As a trader, Soros is known for his bold predictions and courage to make big trades. In fact, Soros is quoted as saying that the biggest error a trader can make is not being bold enough. Soros likes to think deeply about markets and to come up with a thesis that he believes best reflects the world around him. Often he tests the thesis by opening a position in the markets and seeing how it goes, sometimes building it up over months or years. Other times, he likes cutting it quickly if there are losses or if his intuition tells him to sell.

Warren Buffett

Although some might regard the 'Oracle of Omaha' Warren Buffett as more like a buy and hold investor, there is no doubt that he is also a very astute position trader. He may have held stock in some of his favorite companies for several decades but he has also bought and sold many other hundreds of stocks at numerous times throughout his career.

In fact, what most people don't know about Buffett is that he also regularly takes big positions in the derivatives market. He has long held a negative view on gold and has also taken a number of big positions in the bond and forex markets. Indeed, Buffett made around $2bn from a short position in the US dollar in 2005.

All of Warren Buffett's trades have one thing in common: they are all upheld with rigorous economic research and fundamental analysis, leading to macro trends that can span years.

Jim Rogers

Legendary investor, Jim Rogers, co-founded the Quantum Fund with George Soros during its most successful period and famously claims he is not much of a short-term trader, since his timing is always 'too early'. For that reason, Rogers studies markets and the fundamentals before taking positions that generally last anything from a couple of months to a number of years.

Amongst other wins, he successfully predicted the boom in commodities and the 2008 financial crisis even though, in the latter trade, he had to wait for a couple of years for his prediction to come to fruition. Rogers, as a true position trader, is quoted as saying he simply 'waits until there is money lying on the floor, and then goes over and picks it up'.

As Soros, Buffett and Rogers testify there is often far more money to be made in riding out the big trends than by trying to pick the bottoms and tops each day while day trading.

It is for that reason that position trading is good at facilitating big profits. Indeed, it is no wonder that many of the richest traders in the world are all position traders. Big, macroeconomic trends do not come around often but, when they do, they can often lead to huge moves in financial markets over months, years or even decades.

Another reason why position trading is so effective is that market timing becomes less of an issue.

Many traders in the financial world come up with good trading ideas but sometimes they are let down by getting into markets too early or too late. As a result, short-term traders such as day traders need to be watching their screens constantly, since they can lose big money in the space of a couple of minutes if markets turn against them.

Because of this, day traders use a plethora of different techniques in order to try and time markets perfectly.

However, for the position trader, this is much less of a problem. Although there are times when a position trader must react quickly, such as after an unexpected world event, often a position trader has a couple of days, even weeks to initiate or close a position. Big trends are often slow to get going and so a position trader has a lot more flexibility in timing his or her trades. Because of this, position traders have the advantage of not having to watch their screens 24 hours a day, since they are not concerned with daily fluctuations in markets.

It's also easier for a position trader to enter a really big position in a market, and this is why most big funds choose position trading.

Usually, when a really big position is placed in a futures market, that market reacts instantly and in some cases the trade is not filled at the bid price. For a day trader, not hitting the required bid would be a big issue and could cause big losses, but a couple of pips is neither here nor there for a position trader. Thus, large positions are much more easily absorbed into markets over several hours or days. A method that lends itself best to longer-term trading.

There are of course disadvantages to position trading and the biggest is that it is a very long-term strategy. Trades typically take a long time to make any money and trends can last weeks, months or years. That means that a trader must wait a long time to cash in on his profits. They must also have the patience to wait for long periods on the sidelines without putting any money to work.

Which is why many traders choose day trading over longer forms of trading even though it is a much more risky profession.

It is very difficult for a trader with only a small amount of capital to get rich by position trading and would take several years to do so.

Another problem position traders face is the difficulty of manoeuvrability. Since they often have big positions built up in markets, they cannot always get out of them at the flick of a switch. Big positions in illiquid markets can cause problems, since trying to exit markets causes prices to move in an unfavorable direction. This means position traders can be sometimes left vulnerable to big market events and left scrambling to exit their big positions.

Such big events could come in the form of natural disasters or wars, but they may often be caused by the actions of politicians or central banks – those that have big power over markets. It is the central banks that we turn our attention to next.

CENTRAL BANKS

One of the key lessons a trader must learn before attempting to trade is that central banks (such as the Federal Reserve, the Bank of England and the European Central Bank) can have a huge impact on stocks, bonds, commodities, forex and the global economy itself.

Indeed central banks have such power that their actions can cause markets to plummet or soar with just a few carefully worded statements. And, when central banks follow through on their statements with real policies, the price changes can be even more profound. Therefore, if you learn about one thing early on in your trading career, make it central banks.

Such is their importance, that traders must keep a close eye on central banks at all times. They must know when central bankers are due to meet and they must be ready to analyze every word that comes out of their mouths. Central bank meetings (in which bankers meet to discuss inflation expectations and set interest rates) are closely followed events in the investment world and can cause significant volatility in markets.

Just to indicate how important central banks are to financial markets, there are a number of people whose jobs are to solely follow the actions of a particular central bank.

While all central banks are different, most have been vested power by their incumbent nation and usually have the same, simple but important mandate: To promote economic growth while keeping control of inflation. They do this chiefly by controlling interest rates in the economy by purchasing government bonds and other open market securities.

By cutting interest rates central banks seek to make money cheaper to borrow, to increase consumption and, thus, to stimulate the economy, which they do if they think the economy is underperforming. By doing so, they increase the money supply and thereby also increase inflation.

Although it is not always so simple, cutting rates is usually bullish (positive) for the stock market and bearish (negative) for a country's currency, since stocks benefit from the increase in consumption and currency depreciates as a fact of there being a greater supply of that currency.

Similarly, raising rates is generally bearish for stocks and bullish for currency. By limiting the money supply, companies find it harder to borrow and the value of the currency is likely to go up.

Bullish describes the belief that markets will generally rise in price while bearish predicts that markets will fall. For a quick reference guide to financial terms used in this book take a look at the glossary section.

When it comes to central banks around the world the Federal Reserve (the Fed) stands out as the biggest and most influential banking system by a long way. As a provider of liquidity for the United States, the Fed and its chairman Ben Bernanke, control more than $16 trillion dollars. It is the biggest mover of financial markets in the world. To trade successfully, therefore, a trader must know exactly how to respond, whenever the Fed makes its next move.

The characteristics of central banks

As I've said, central banks, particularly the Fed, have the most power in guiding the direction of nearly every asset class.

By cutting rates aggressively or by using strategies such as quantitative easing, central banks can inject liquidity into the economy, propelling stocks to new highs and depreciating the value of currencies. Similarly, by raising rates, they can curb inflation and cause currencies to go up in value.

However, not all central banks have the same power and each one, as we shall find, has its own distinct personality.

Knowing the different characteristics of each bank is essential in order to predict what they might do next.

The Federal Reserve – The Speed Boat
Head: Ben Bernanke (soon to be Janet Yellen)

As controller of the biggest economy in the world (the United States), the Fed is by far the most influential central bank and its policies are able to affect not just the US economy but the global economy as a whole. As such, Chairman of the Fed, Ben Bernanke, has one of the most powerful jobs in the world.

The best way to describe the Fed when compared to other central banks is by way of a speed boat. The Fed is always fast to act and quick to respond to changes in the economy. It sees itself as entrepreneurial, much like the American people, and it has little problem changing direction if the situation needs it.

For example, during the financial crisis in 2008, the Fed responded by cutting rates to near zero. The Fed is nearly always the first to act and be aggressive in its approach. This is good to remember whenever the Fed meets to talk or to set rates, (which it does once a month). As a trader, never bet against the Fed making another bold move and be prepared to react when it does.

European Central Bank – The Oil Tanker
Head: Mario Draghi

Although the European economy as a whole is about as big as the United States economy, the European Central Bank (ECB) is not as big an influence on the world stage as the Fed.

The ECB typically has less control over its policies as a result of being responsible to so many different country nations (including Germany) and is therefore a lot slower in its policy moves. In fact, if we say that the Fed is a speed boat then we can refer to the ECB as being an oil tanker. Big and cumbersome, the ECB has come under criticism at times for being too slow to respond to economic crises and for being behind the curve. This was partly seen in 2008 when it actually raised rates shortly before the global meltdown.

Unlike the Fed, the ECB's principle mandate is to control inflation and it sets its target at 2%. In many ways, the ECB's negativity towards inflation is a reaction to the dark days of Nazi Germany when hyperinflation caused so much damage making it almost understandable that the ECB continues this vigilance. All in all, the ECB is generally slow to act and unlikely to make any rash decisions when it comes to setting policy.

Although the ECB tends to not be as aggressive as the Fed, their lack of action can be just as important to future price moves as anything else, so it pays to always understand what is going on before the ECB meets or before one of the ECB's members speaks.

Bank of England – The Ocean Liner
Head: Mark Carney

The Bank of England (BOE) is made up of the monetary policy committee (MPC) and is arguably the third most powerful central bank in the world. It is responsible for controlling liquidity and stimulating growth in the United Kingdom's economy and the MPC meets once a month to decide on policy action. Like the ECB, the BOE also has an inflation target of 2% but it is far less tied to it than the ECB. The BOE often lets inflation go a little higher than the target if it sees the economy struggling and it makes strong policy moves if it sees fit, such as cutting rates or expanding the balance sheet. Although it is not as aggressive as the Fed, the BOE is quicker to respond than the ECB and more willing to take risks.

People's Bank of China – The Hovercraft
Head: Zhou Xiaochaun

As the country's central bank, the People's Bank of China (PBC) is becoming ever more important on a global stage. In fact, it is the biggest financial institution in the world when measured in terms of the financial assets it holds.

As China's economy has grown in recent years, the PBC has maintained a strong strategy of accumulating large quantities of US treasuries and precious metals such as gold and this is likely to see the bank in good stead for the future.

Although some of the bank's powers are spread to other offices, the PBC has shown itself to be quick to respond to market events and has made some smart policy measures such as those designed to cool China's property bubble. However, by not allowing its currency to be freely exchangeable, the bank is still a bit behind the times.

The rest

There are many other important central banks on the world stage including the Bank of Japan, the Reserve Bank of Australia and the Central Bank of Brazil, with the Bank of Japan in particular, becoming considerably more aggressive in recent months.

Although these are the most important banks it is worth remembering that the action of any central bank, no matter how small, can have a big effect on a market such as the national currency of that country. Their actions should always be considered.

KEYNES: MACROECONOMICS AND EXPECTATIONS

After following the financial markets for a short while, it will not be long before you begin to form judgements over the decisions made by various policy makers. Since the financial crisis in 2008, there has been mixed reaction (to say the least) at the decisions made by politicians and central bank officials.

Much of the commentary has been negative. Central banks have been criticised by many for bailing out failed financial institutions and implementing the biggest program of monetary easing in recorded history.

To understand why central banks, such as the Fed, have cut rates to zero, instigated huge programs of quantitative easing and blown up the budget deficit to unprecedented levels, it is necessary to know a little bit about the late British economist, John Maynard Keynes.

Keynes

Keynes was a British economist whose ideas rose to significance during the 1930s Depression era, and again after the Second World War. He proposed that macroeconomics was fundamentally concerned with three things: the output of an economy, inflation, and expectations.

After the Second World War, the success of Keynesian economics caused the mainstream of American economists to adopt Keynesian ideas. This explains a great deal why the Fed has acted in the way it has in recent times. Knowing Keynesian economics also helps to predict how the Fed will act in the future.

The Great Depression

During the 1930s, the United States and much of the world entered a prolonged economic depression that saw the Dow Jones lose 89% of its value.

What is surprising, is that many economists and politicians at the time were at a loss as to why this was happening.

The States experienced no fall in labour or industrial resource that should have led to such a determined downward spiral in economic conditions.

At the time, President Roosevelt proclaimed, "Our distress comes from no failure of substance. We are stricken by no plague of locusts…Plenty is at our doorstep but a generous use of it languishes in the very sight of supply."

Keynes said that the reason for the downturn was not to do with supply (since America did not lack resource or economic will) but rather one of demand. Moreover, Keynes argued that negative expectations (or 'animal spirits' as he called them) had become self-fulfilling, so that demand had also plummeted.

He argued that if expectations of future growth were bad enough, employers and business owners would withhold investments, while consumers would put money aside instead of spending it.

The result would be a vicious cycle of reduced output and prolonged economic woe. A situation that, if bad enough, could not be resolved by even aggressive monetary loosening by central banks.

Keynes came to the conclusion that when expectations become so entrenched that they lead to severe economic recession or depression, policymakers should do everything in their power in order to bring output back to its potential level.

Central banks should drive interest rates down as far as possible (by controlling money supply) and governments should run large budget deficits in order to encourage further spending.

Keynes proposed a model known as an income 'multiplier' which explained why an increasing budget deficit would eventually lead to a more than proportionate rise in GDP.

Put simply, Keynes said that a rise in government spending would result in a bigger proportionate rise in national income as further consumer spending and investment went back into the economy. Keynes estimated that increased government spending could equate to an increase in national income, by a factor of five times as much.

In other words, if the government increased spending by $100, the overall benefit to the economy would equate to a GDP of as much as $500.

Taking these steps, Keynes said it should therefore be possible to reverse expectations enough so that markets become self-fulfilling once more. This time, by encouraging future investment and spending, leading to the resurgence of output within the economy and restarting the business cycle.

Overheating

As the economy recovers to its potential, Keynes suggested that inflation also ignites, as a result of the increase in money supply. When this occurs, officials should act quickly to control the inflation before the economy overheats. They should do so by reversing the methods used to ignite growth in the first place. In other words, by reducing spending and raising rates. If they don't, inflation has the potential to run away to unsustainable and dangerous levels.

The present day

Today, it is quite clear that central banks have taken a Keynesian approach to tackling the financial crisis. In 2008, what started as a housing bubble in America quickly led to severe contractions in output across the world. As negative expectations became entrenched, banks stopped lending to each other and sparked fears of bank runs and further crises.

The Fed responded by driving interest rates to near zero and buying up government bonds on a huge scale. By 2012, the US government was running a budget deficit of over $1 trillion dollars (6.3% of GDP).

Inflation is yet to really ignite in the States (as of November 2013, US inflation stood at around 1.6%). But when it does, you can be sure that the Fed will work quickly to turn off the printing presses and fulfil the next part of the Kenynesian ideal. Savvy traders will be on the lookout for such an event, well before it occurs.

WHAT IS INFLATION?

Inflation is the rise in prices of goods and services in an economy and having an understanding of it is essential in order to trade financial markets effectively. Deflation on the other hand, occurs when prices experience an overall decline and normally occurs during periods of economic struggle.

Inflation has been practised throughout history as a tool that governments use to pay for its expenses, spur economic growth and control the populace of a country. Historically, governments would induce inflation by melting down gold coins and mixing them with other metals such as silver, copper or lead.

The government could thus issue more coins, at the same nominal value, effectively putting more coins into the money supply and diluting the real value of each coin. The effect of this is that the government can produce the same value money at a cheaper cost. The government is therefore able to gather more money to finance its expenses.

As the distribution of money increases, the populace feels more content as they believe (incorrectly) that they are becoming wealthier.

These days, governments are able to increase money supply much more easily by printing paper money, also known as fiat currency.

You need to know about inflation and deflation in order to understand what kinds of returns you should be targeting and what sort of returns may or may not be possible.

If inflation is high, then your returns need to be equally high or you are not making any money.

For example, let's say that inflation was 3% last year but your portfolio only returned 2%.

In other words, even though your portfolio made 2%, you still lost money in real terms, since the prices of everything around you has gone up more than your wealth has. Similarly, if your investment makes 3% and inflation is also at 3%, you are no better off.

Generally, economists favor a level of inflation that is low and steady, around 2%. Much lower than that and economists fear stagnation while much higher and the implications from an economic slow-down become more severe. Central banks, therefore, use interest rates to try and keep inflation at around this 2% mark.

Any return you make must always be compared to the rate of inflation. Generally, when prices are dropping it is harder to make bigger returns so look for investments that are immune to low prices and benefit from lower interest rates. Investments such as banks and bonds, for example. Conversely, if prices are forecast to rise, look to investments that retain their value, such as property, gold or commodity stocks.

THE TYPICAL MARKET CYCLE

Good traders know that central banks have huge influence over the outcome of financial markets but it is the market cycle and real economics that ultimately drives prices. The stock market is a big influence, since it is arguably the market that is most clearly affected by changes in economic fundamentals.

Financial markets are always interconnected with one another, so no matter what asset you trade you must have a clear understanding of the outlook for the stock market. One way to do this is to have a sound understanding of a typical market cycle.

1. Coming to the end of the market cycle

During the latter stages of a bull market, such as experienced in 1999 and 2007, there is typically strong economic growth and high levels of optimism among market participants. It is during this time that the market cycle nears its peak. Consumer confidence is likely high, interest rates rise and cyclical stocks begin to outperform. It is not always the case, but these are the usual characteristics of a maturing market.

As markets move up, rising interest rates become an ever stronger threat to economic growth and markets begin to slow in momentum. Lending money becomes more expensive and thus risk taking begins to drop, leading to investors seeking more secure places to invest – such as utility and value stocks.

This in turn leads to sharp falls in the growth stocks that were previously in charge and mounting pessimism begins to set in as the main driver. As pessimism increases, economic growth begins to fall and small cap stocks and growth stocks bear most of the pain.

In order to address the decline in growth, interest rates start to fall and the stock market most likely enters a prolonged bear market. Traders begin to sell higher yielding investments and move into safer investments such as bonds, utility stocks or safe havens.

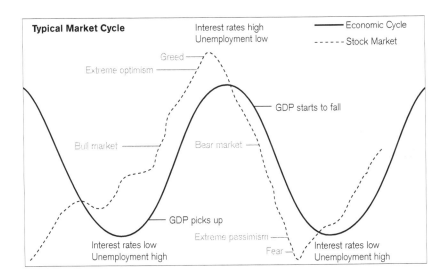

2. Restarting the market cycle

As interest rates fall and pessimism takes hold, markets keep dropping until they reach a selling climax, where optimism is at its lowest. It is at this point when markets are washed out and at their lowest ebb that the cycle can begin again. Fuelled by the prospect of now low interest rates, and improving economic growth, small cap stocks and growth stocks take over and markets start to rise.

Since the stock market looks ahead, this rise is often happening well in advance of any corresponding uptick in GDP or unemployment. In this way, the stock market is the ultimate leading indicator into future economic growth.

It is important to understand the market cycle. Although no cycle is ever the same, it is generally the case that riskier assets and small cap stocks do better in the beginning stages of bull markets. Whereas in bear markets, bonds and defensive stocks do better. As do safe-haven currencies such as the US dollar, the Swiss franc and the Japanese yen.

ASSESSING MARKET CYCLES USING INDICATORS

Understanding current market cycles aids in timing markets. But since cycles can go on for a number of years and each one is different, it is not always easy to ascertain what stage we are at. Fortunately, a closer examination of various economic indicators can help form a top down view of which stage of the market cycle we are currently in.

Another reason why economic indicators should be given attention is that by understanding economic conditions you are in a much better place to anticipate future policy decisions by central banks such as the Fed.

Money supply and the yield curve

Money supply

Money supply, by and large, increases as an economy worsens and slows as a market cycle nears its peak. It is controlled by central banks and in the States the Fed can control the money supply by changing its reserve rate requirement.

The principle way it does this is by changing the Fed target rate, which it is able to keep in place by buying and selling US government securities in the open market at the required rate. This process is known as an open market operation and, while there are several other methods the bank uses to control money supply, this is the main one.

Generally, traders use the economic indicators M2 and M3 to measure money supply in the economy and these numbers are released regularly by the Fed. M1 used to be used but these days it is subject to too many distortions for accurate analysis. (I have included with this book a number of spreadsheets, including money supply data, which you can analyze at your convenience).

If you regularly keep track of money supply you should also be able to predict long-term shifts in interest rates.

When money supply is shooting up, inflation is likely to follow which then has to be controlled by higher interest rates. For traders, this means currency yields in the US increase while the US dollar itself likely depreciates. Stocks, in theory, should benefit from an increase in money supply, as do commodities, particularly precious metals.

Yield curve

We have seen how money supply can affect interest rates but we should also look closely at interest rates themselves – in particular the difference between long-term rates and shorter-term T-Bills (known as the yield curve).

The yield curve reacts to dynamics in cash markets and is an extremely useful guide to the future of the economy. You can view it in real time by logging on to any one of the main finance websites, such as Bloomberg.com, and calculate it for yourself using some of the spreadsheets provided within this book.

When long-term rates are much higher than short-term rates, the yield curve is steep and indicates an optimistic environment. The

Fed is typically accommodative, stock prices typically do well and markets expect an improving economy.

Conversely, the yield curve can be said to be flat, or inverted, when short-term rates are close to or above longer-term rates. This occurs when markets expect economic weakness, and longer-term rates are deemed too risky. It is a scenario often accompanied by a restrictive Fed and a certain level of fear and pessimism in the financial markets.

It makes sense to follow the yield curve as it can be a useful leading indicator in the state of the market. By and large, a steep yield curve means economic growth which should benefit riskier assets such as stocks, while a flat or inverted yield curve means traders should be prepared to shift into safer haven markets. The yield curve is one of the best leading indicators available to traders and contains brilliant insight into the functioning of the money markets.

INVESTING IN MONEY MARKETS

As we have seen, central banks are perhaps the biggest influence on financial markets. One of the reasons for this, is their ability to control money markets that financial institutions use to fund their daily activities.

In general, central banks aim to provide stability to markets and encourage lending between financial institutions. We saw in 2008 the problems that can occur when banks stop lending money to each other (for fear of losses) as the London Interbank Offered Rate (LIBOR) went up.

LIBOR is the estimated interest rate offered between leading banks in London and is a key component of the TED spread; a name formed from the merging of T-Bill and ED, the ticker symbol for the Eurodollar futures contract.

Essentially, the TED spread is the difference between the three-month LIBOR and the three-month risk-free T-Bill rate. This spread came to be a good indicator of fear during the financial crisis.

An increase in the TED is therefore a sign that the risk of default on loans between banks is increasing. If banks are fearful of lending to each other it means they are worried about their solvency and is a worrying prospect for the financial system.

The long-term average of the TED spread is a difference of around 30 basis points, but during the financial crisis the indicator ballooned to 457. The TED also jumped higher during the 1987 crash.

Money market funds

Investing in a money market fund is like putting your money in a big pool of secure, highly liquid short-term debt securities, the same pool of money as described above that the big institutions use to keep money overnight before deploying elsewhere.

It's important to note that money market funds differ from money market deposit accounts. Whereas money market funds are investment vehicles that the investor picks for his own investment, money market deposit accounts are investments where the bank receives the funds and can invest the cash at its own discretion.

The whole point of a money market fund is to be a secure place to store money so that the value of the fund never drops below the net asset value (NAV) of $1. As such, money market funds generally offer safe returns at rates a little bit higher than checking accounts.

Nevertheless, money market funds can lose money on rare occasions and are not insured by the Federal Deposit Insurance Company (FDIC).

Breaking the buck

Money market funds rarely lose investors' money but when they do, it is referred to as breaking the buck, as the fund drops below the NAV of $1. Prior to 2008, there was only one instance of a money market fund breaking the buck and that was an institutional fund that paid out at 96 cents for every dollar invested.

In 2008, after Lehman Brothers went bankrupt, another money market fund broke the buck with its value falling to 97 cents per share. The amount of money invested in money market funds at the time meant that a single fund breaking the buck could have led to ripple effects and cause a potential run on banks. Because of this, the Fed stepped in and guaranteed funding to protect public money market funds from slipping below $1.

The Fed came to the rescue in 2008 but it may not always do so going forward. Therefore, it's still important for the investor to do their due diligence before investing.

On the whole though, money market funds are secure and there are several factors that make them safe places to store money:

1. Money market funds typically only invest in high quality AAA grade debt;

2. They're not allowed to invest more than 5% of the fund in one issuer (except the government), which means the risk is spread across several firms;

3. Money market funds have an average weighted portfolio maturity of less than 90 days. This means managers have a lot of room to manage the risks of certain securities.

The biggest risk with money market funds typically comes from extraordinary long tail events where credit conditions change dramatically in a short space of time. Rapid shifts in overnight lending rates between banks or sudden movements in interest rates can put pressure on some money market funds that are concentrated in the wrong areas. It is therefore important for the investor to seek out the details of a money market fund before committing any investment.

Particular attention should be paid to the current macro-economic environment and the health of the banking sector. In general, money market funds from the bigger institutions provide lower risk as they are more heavily capitalized and better able to ride out extreme market volatility.

Like money market funds, bonds also react directly to changes in money supply. Although not as secure as money market funds, they are among the safest investments in the financial community. Because of their perceived security, bonds take up a huge role in the financial system.

INVESTING IN BONDS

Bonds, in their myriad of forms, are among the least understood investments but they can provide a steady, reliable stream of income as well as being secure places to park one's money – particularly when expected returns on riskier assets such as stocks is uncertain.

Bonds are essentially IOUs. You lend money to a company or institution for a certain amount of time; in return, you receive interest and the money you lent in full at the end of the loan, called the maturity date. You can also sell your bond early. If the value of the bond goes up, you can bank the capital gained on your investment.

The key thing to remember is that bonds move in the opposite direction of interest rates. When rates fall, bonds rise and vice versa.

All bonds have a par price of 100 and go up or down depending on interest rates. So if you buy a bond at 100 with a yield of 3% and rates go down enough so that your bond goes up in value to 105, you earn 3% per year in interest as well as bank 5% capital gain if you sell it. If rates go up, you still get the 3% but receive your money back in full at the end of the term without any gain.

There are essentially three different types of bonds.

The first two are both investment grade bonds and are provided by governments, agencies, cities, corporations or states.

Government bonds provide possibly the safest investments available and, because of this, garner much lower rates of return. The reason why they are so safe is that governments are much less likely to go bankrupt than other entities such as companies. (If they do get into trouble they can always raise taxes from their citizens to pay back the debt.)

That is not to say governments never default on their debt of course and explains why certain countries (for example Greece and Argentina) offer much higher yields than other countries like Germany.

Corporate bonds provide higher yearly returns but there is always a chance of the company going into liquidation and defaulting on the debt.

The other types of bonds are referred to as Junk bonds. These riskier bonds are below investment grade. As such, they generate yet higher returns on investment.

An easy way to see the level of risk associated with a certain bond is by looking at the ratings provided by rating agencies such as Fitch and Moody's. Bonds are rated from AAA down to D where D denotes an imminent default is likely.

Such ratings, however, must be taken with a pinch of salt. The rating agencies came under intense pressure in 2008 for their part in the financial crisis as they maintained AAA ratings of bonds that were ultimately worthless. Ratings agencies often have a conflict of interest in that the companies that pay for their services are the same companies that the agencies must rate and they are often much slower than the markets to downgrade risky bonds.

When investing in bonds, an investor therefore needs to consider a number of different scenarios.

If capital preservation and reliable income is all that is needed then secure bonds such as US Treasuries can provide that answer.

For more risk adverse investors looking to secure not only income but also gains on their capital, an opinion on the outlook for interest rates and the future implications for inflation is needed.

With interest rates at historic lows and central banks seemingly doing everything in their favor to stoke economic growth, long-term investment in bonds is not the best investment at the present time. Bonds may perform adequately for a short period of time but there is a danger of them becoming the next bubble.

If you are worried over inflation but like the security of a bond, treasury inflation protected securities (TIPS) are a good buy as they improve when interest rates rise – the opposite of normal bonds.

Bonds are also good instruments to trade with due to their high liquidity and many traders specialize in day trading US 10-year bonds and German Bunds. The skills needed for trading bonds are just the same as for trading stocks or commodities. The same principles exist across different markets, however, bond traders need to pay extra attention to interest rates and inflation of course. Bond auctions can also be good indicators of the demand for a particular bond.

HOW THE TRADE BALANCE AFFECTS CURRENCY PRICES

Predicting the direction of forex markets is notoriously difficult. In fact, there are many people in the academic world who believe it to be almost impossible – at least on a short-term basis.

On longer time frames, there is more agreement. Many of those who study macroeconomics believe that the trick to predicting where a currency might go is to look at a country's current account balance.

The current account balance is the sum of the balance of trade, factor income and cash transfers – where factor income means earnings on foreign investments minus payments to foreign investors. It basically describes the flow of money between two countries.

Supply and demand

Macroeconomic theory dictates that a country's currency is subject to the same laws of supply and demand as any other asset. If a currency is in greater demand it becomes worth more, whereas if it is greater in supply, it depreciates.

To understand this, consider a country whose inhabitants develop a strong urge to buy products from a foreign country. In this situation, the act of buying foreign goods increases the demand for the foreign currency, since that is what the goods are priced in. At the same time, the current account balance of the country deteriorates, as more imports are coming in compared to exports.

The result is a trade deficit and a depreciation of the native currency since it is in much less demand.

However, there are other scenarios too.

Consider for example, a country whose financial products, such as bonds, become wanted by foreign investors. In this case, the current account balance also deteriorates (as a result of negative cash transfers), but the currency goes up in value instead of down. Since the increase in demand for the country's financial assets means an increase in demand for its currency.

Longer term outlook

Economists tend to disagree on just how easily the current account balance can be used to predict foreign exchange prices. However, it is generally thought that sustained current account deficits lead to a depreciation in a country's currency, while prolonged current account surpluses lead to appreciation. It is thought too, that a current account deficit larger than 5 (as a percentage of GDP) is unsustainable and a potential warning sign for a country.

Take a look at the current account deficits for various countries and you see that for the majority of developed countries, the current account deficit is lower than 5.

While it would be extremely difficult to use such data to trade forex markets in the short-term the current account balance can provide some use for predicting markets over longer term horizons.

The data can be freely found online and it is also released monthly by governments. One idea is to use the current account balance as one factor in the development of an indicator. Such an indicator can be used to decide which side of the market to trade on; long or short.

Interest rates and forex

Interest rates, or more importantly – the expectations of future interest rates – are probably the most significant factors that influence forex markets in the short to medium term.

The reason for this, is that market participants naturally move their money towards those currencies with the highest yields, as those yields give the best return for their money. Therefore, those countries with the higher interest rates see much larger inflows of money coming into their currencies.

As a general rule then, countries with higher rates should see their currency appreciate while those countries with lower rates should see their currency weaken.

However, as noted above, the real key to predicting forex markets is identifying where interest rates are headed before they go there. Since, by the time a country has raised interest rates, that decision is likely already priced into the markets (and that country's currency has already become stronger).

It's important therefore, to recognize market expectations as a key driver for all forex pairs.

For example, if interest rates drop for a while and traders suddenly decide that they have hit bottom, they begin to buy up the currency, well in advance of interest rates going up. In fact, sometimes the very act of traders changing their market views can alter the economic environment enough to influence future outcomes.

It is, therefore, important to understand news releases and economic reports as they can change the sentiment among traders, even if the opinion among central banks remains the same. Equally, it is just as likely for markets to price in events that do not end up transpiring in real life.

Let's look at the most recent FOMC policy meeting whereby the Fed's governor Ben Bernanke went against market expectations and kept current levels of QE unchanged at $85bn per month.

Running up to the event, markets had become convinced that Bernanke would 'taper' asset purchases, so much so that traders sold down stocks and bought up the US dollar. (Since tapering reduces money supply this act would in theory be bullish, and deflationary, for the US dollar.)

However, Bernanke surprised the markets and did not taper. The result saw stocks advance and the US dollar give up most of its gains in a short time, as traders reacted once more to the change in expectations.

The funny thing is, Bernanke had not actually given any indication that he would taper in the last meeting, but a series of positive economic releases had convinced traders that he would. As you can see, most of the time it pays to move with market sentiment. However, in certain instances, like the example above, it can pay even more to go against market sentiment, when there is enough risk/reward in doing so.

GETTING STARTED IN BONDS, STOCKS, FOREX AND COMMODITIES

Bonds

Getting started in bonds depends on the type of bond you want to buy, where you live and how much money you have.

Government bonds can be bought from any of the big brokerages and banks. Some can also be bought direct from the US Treasury or from a regional Federal Reserve Bank. Their prices and ratings can be easily accessed through financial news websites, such as the Financial Times and the Wall Street Journal, or through one of the rating agency websites.

It is also possible to invest in bonds by buying bond futures through a broker or through an ETF that tracks bonds prices, such as the iShares 1-3 Year Treasury Bond ETF, for example.

For short-term trading, US 10-year notes, UK Gilts (United Kingdom government bonds) and German Bunds are all highly liquid government bonds that can be traded as futures via a stockbroker, a contract for difference (CFD) provider or using a respectable spread betting firm if in the UK.

Stocks

Stocks can be bought via any stockbroker with many investment banks and online brokers offering this service. The Internet has brought down the costs of investing in stocks with many brokers such as E*Trade Financial, TradeMonster and Scottrade offering fixed commissions of around $10 per trade for stocks and $4 for futures. TradeMonster also offers an unlimited demo period to try out your trading ideas.

You can also trade stocks via a CFD provider or spread betting firm with similarly low commissions, or you can buy an ETF that tracks stock prices.

Short-term trading in stocks is better suited to the main indices, since the costs are even lower. The most popular stock indices to trade are as follows:

United States:

Dow Jones Industrial Average

S&P 500

Nasdaq (Technology)

Europe:

FTSE 100 (UK)

DAX (Germany)

CAC (France)

Asia/Australasia:

Nikkei (Japan)

Hang Seng (Hong Kong)

ASX (Australia)

Commodities, forex and ETFs

Most brokerages these days cater for the whole gamut of investment products so the same brokers that sell you stocks usually sell you commodities futures, currencies and ETFs too. A list of ETFs can be found at www.Bloomberg.com under 'Market Data', 'ETFs'.

In terms of coverage, Interactive Brokers is a well-respected brokerage site that pretty much does it all.

The Internet has really brought down much of the cost of investing in all of these products, so deciding on which broker to use usually comes down to a matter of time frames.

Typically, stock brokers are more aligned to investing and suit longer time frames whereas for shorter-term trading it's cheaper to use a futures broker, CFD provider or spread bettor. A full list of brokers and trading platforms can be found in the Resources section.

CHAPTER 2:
TIMING

METHODS TO TIME THE MARKET

The 1980s and '90s were such good times for stocks that many people became wealthy without having to know a thing about investing. A simple buy and hold strategy, with no thought towards market timing was all that was needed to reap the rewards that came with being invested in the world's largest economy.

However, the same strategy implemented over the last 13 years, would not have performed so well with the Dow Jones industrial average currently sitting only slightly higher than where it was at the turn of the century.

Professional investors know that to navigate the markets effectively it is essential to have more than one strategy to time the market.

The famous Wall Street adage, 'buy low and sell high' may well be a favorite among stock brokers and commentators, but just what does constitute as low, and what as high?

The correct answer is that there are more than a couple of ways to ascertain whether something is cheap or not. As we shall see, there is an art to investing as well as a science.

1. Financial ratios

Financial ratios are generally used to provide bottom up analysis of individual stocks and the various statistics can be found on any good finance website, such as Yahoo! or Google Finance.

Price/earnings

The price/earnings ratio (P/E) is probably the most popular method traders use to value a stock. P/E is the price of a stock divided by its earnings over the last year. So if a company is priced at $30 and has earnings last year of $3, the company has a P/E of 10.

Historically, companies have averaged a P/E of around 15, so in theory, stocks with P/Es lower than this can be considered cheap.

However, buying a company because of a low P/E is a flawed strategy since it takes no account of future earnings. Indeed, many companies with high P/E's go on to be great investments. Google, for instance, has a P/E of 24.6. Likewise, stocks with low P/Es can often be in stale industries and not make much progress either.

A better strategy is to use the ratio and combine it with other factors such as projected growth, debt to equity, earnings per share or statistics from other areas of the company's finances – such as its balance sheet. But projected growth is the real key, since trading in a stock is all about what it will deliver in the future, not what it has done in the past.

Earnings per share

Earnings per share (EPS) describes the profit of a company allocated to each outstanding stock and is calculated as:

EPS = net income - dividends on preferred stock / average outstanding shares.

It is an important indicator and is useful for comparing companies. If two companies have the same EPS but one has a lower level of equity or investment, it can be said that that company is more efficient. However, the problem with EPS is that it can easily be manipulated by cunning accountants so it is important to use it in conjunction with other metrics.

Price/earnings to growth

Price/earnings to growth (PEG) is calculated by dividing the P/E ratio by annual EPS growth. It therefore aims to improve on the P/E ratio by taking into account future earnings. A PEG below 1 is preferable although it is also important to consider what has been used to measure the growth. It is also important to take into account the P/E ratios that exist across that specific industry.

Debt to equity

The debt to equity ratio is measured by dividing total liabilities by shareholders equity and is a good indicator of leverage. Generally a high debt to equity ratio means a company has been aggressive in financing which could lead to volatile earnings. However, debt to equity levels generally differ across markets and industries so this needs to be taken into account. Not all debt is bad, but too much debt can be dangerous.

Price to book ratio

Value investors often use the price to book ratio as it compares the share price to an estimate of the value of the company. It is calculated as:

Price to book ratio = Share price / total assets–intangible assets and liabilities.

Generally, this ratio tells you how much the company would be worth if it was sold off as-is. A lower number is therefore preferable. However, a low number could also indicate something fundamentally wrong with the company so it should be combined with other factors too.

Current ratio

Current ratio is measured by dividing current assets by current liabilities, and is a good indicator of liquidity. Generally, the higher liquidity within the company the better, as it means a company is in a better position to pay off debts. However, a current ratio that is too high could indicate that a company is hoarding cash and not reinvesting in the business. Although this is not necessarily an issue if market conditions are deteriorating sufficiently.

There are plenty of different ratios that investors use to analyze stocks and these are just a handful of the most important ones. Not all ratios are useful and many depend on the stock itself or the industry it operates in. One way around this is to form a composite indicator to combine ratios. This method can greatly help in screening for the best value stocks.

I have provided with this book a useful Excel Spreadsheet from www.investexcel.net that can be used to calculate how cheap a stock is.

Shiller CAPE ratio

Another method which is useful for overall market timing is to use the Shiller CAPE ratio which measures valuation for the broader market and stands for the cyclically-adjusted P/E ratio. It is a better measure for P/E valuation, as it measures the previous 10 years of earnings of S&P 500 companies adjusted for inflation using the consumer price index.

Values below historical norms such as 14 indicate markets are cheap and these are generally good times to buy. Since many stocks move in-line with the indices most of the time, this can be a nice method for timing investments, and the Shiller P/E stands up against data going back to the early 1900s. As of October 2013, the Shiller P/E ratio sits above 23 so the stock market is considered expensive on this measure.

To see a live recording of the Shiller P/E, visit GuruFocus' site, www.gurufocus.com/shiller-PE.php

2. Balance sheet

A company's balance sheet, like its cash flow, offers a snapshot into the health of a company at a given point in time and is a good tool to measure a company's value. The balance sheet essentially measures what a company has or expects to get (assets) and what it owes to others (liabilities). Companies with high levels of debt tend to be the most volatile investments.

As a shareholder or investor, this ratio between assets and liabilities is key, since it is the value of all those assets when liquidated that provides the ultimate value of the business. A company that generates more cash than it needs to fund its operations is going to add value to its stock and is likely to climb. Additionally, such a company would likely give some of its excess cash back to shareholders in the form of share buybacks or dividends.

With careful analysis it is possible to find some real surprises in balance sheets that can lead to big stock moves. Sometimes those surprises can lead to a company going under or even being investigated for fraud, such as what happened with Enron. For a good book that deals with finding accounting irregularities, check out The Art of Short Selling by Kathryn Stanley.

3. Market cycle

We looked briefly at the market cycle in the last chapter and basic economics teaches us that when something is very cheap people buy it. In turn that reduces the supply and therefore increases the price of whatever the thing is. Subsequently, new suppliers come to market in order to take advantage of the high prices which, in turn, increases the supply, eventually causing prices to fall back again. This is especially true for commodities but also works for stocks.

All markets work like this and operate in cycles spanning from a few years to long 20 to 30-year bull and bear runs. This means that major 20 to 30-year bull or bear markets are actually a typical occurrence as it can take long periods of time for new suppliers to come to markets.

Historically, it is rare for a major bull or bear market to last longer than that, so if you find a market that has been going down for 20-30 years and has finally started to stabilize, it may indicate the market is very cheap and ready for a new bull cycle.

4. Scan a chart

While a market's cycle can be measured relatively objectively, there is also value in scanning the historical price chart of a security. It is a fast and easy way to quickly tell whether something is depressed (or not) and if it can be the starting ground for further research.

Look for charts where the price has been hovering at historically low prices for a couple of years or more; it is a fair bet that a decent bottom has formed. Once you've found a stock that looks like it may have bottomed do some more research into the company. Have a look at its finances. If it has something to offer from a fundamental point of view, it can be an even stronger trade.

5. Relative Graham Value

Benjamin Graham, author of Security Analysis, formulated the relative Graham value (RGV) – a measure which has been modified to great affect by famous value investors such as Warren Buffet. The strategy states that stocks fluctuate around their intrinsic value over time with the original formula for intrinsic value described as:

$IV = [EPS \times (8.5 + 2G)] \times (4.4 / Y)$

Where:

IV = Intrinsic value

EPS = Projected 12-month earnings per share

8.5 = appropriate P/E for a no growth company according to Benjamin Graham

G = company's 5-year earnings growth estimate

4.4 = average yield of high-grade corporate bonds

Y = current yield on AAA 30 year corporate bonds

All of these statistics can be easily found online at a site like Yahoo! Finance or Finviz.com

The theory states that when a stock trades below its intrinsic value it is cheap and when it trades above it is expensive. The formula is noted for its simplicity but it is a good first level check to see whether a stock is cheap or not.

Graham goes on to state that a 25% margin of safety is a good rule of thumb when investing in a business that is below its intrinsic value. The greater the margin of safety the better the investment.

Try your own

RGV is one example of a valuation method that, when combined with some extra criteria, has worked to great affect for several notable investors, including Warren Buffett. But there is nothing to stop you from coming up with your own investment criteria.

You can get creative here and come up with a strategy of your choice, using the metrics you discern. Balance sheet calculations, earnings ratios and even qualitative methods can be used. By forming your own composite metrics you may be able to get away from the crowd and make even stronger investment decisions. Decisions that are unlikely to have been copied elsewhere.

Try back-testing your ideas on historical stock market data and you might be able to come up with a winning strategy of your own.

ADVANCED TIMING METHODS

The methods discussed so far are pretty standard ways to time the markets and work well over medium to long-term time frames using freely available economic data.

But what if your focus is on other metrics and different time frames? In such situations it may be necessary to look at more advanced methods to sharpen your timing skills.

Volatility

Volatility is one method professionals use to make market timing a little bit easier. Without exception, the best time to buy stocks is when volatility is at its peak in the stock market.

High levels of volatility have coincided with all the major bear market troughs such as in 1930, 1987 and 2008. Find a period of high volatility and you also find a major bottom.

Professionals often use a measure called the VIX – a trademarked ticker symbol for the Chicago Board Options Exchange Market Volatility Index, a popular measure to estimate the volatility in markets. High levels of volatility typically signal good buying points and low levels are often good places to sell.

While it is not always easy to tell when a market becomes more volatile, a good rule of thumb is to become more aggressive when volatility increases above its historical 2-year average. Historically, this has been a good guide, but always be aware that periods of high or low volatility can persist for longer than you would think.

Dow theory

Dow Theory, developed by Charles H. Dow in the late 19th century, is also a popular strategy to find peaks and troughs in markets; and amazingly, is still used by professionals today. The basic principle cites that markets go through a number of phases.

First, investors latch on to the fact that markets are cheap and start accumulating stocks. This in turn causes the stock market to go up and continues on until nearly everyone in the market is aware of it. It is at this point that rampant speculation takes over, resulting in rapid price change. Once this period of speculation is exhausted, astute investors realize the speculation is overdone and begin to dissolve their holdings, which itself often leads to rapid selling.

While it isn't the purpose of this book to go into the details of the Dow Theory, knowing these different market phases can offer a good introduction into the way markets operate and how to take advantage of them. The essence of the Dow Theory, which is to try and buy when people are unaware of something and sell before rampant speculation is exhausted, remains sound.

Sentiment indicators

As well as using time-old methods such as Dow Theory, professionals look at sentiment indicators. In fact, consumer sentiment and investor sentiment surveys are given a lot of consideration by some investors. So much so, the results of such surveys are often sold for thousands of dollars to banks and hedge funds.

The reason for this is that professional traders like to buy stocks when there is fear and sell when people are greedy. By monitoring the sentiment of market participants, as well as the general public, they are better able to analyze this information in a quantitative way.

Indicators provided by advisory services, such as Investors Intelligence or Barrons, are excellent measures of public opinion and gauge the number of bulls or bears in markets. When there is extreme pessimism, it is often a great time to buy stocks. Similarly, when optimism abounds, the best thing to do is to sell. Increasingly, savvy investors are looking to newer ways to gauge sentiment such as with social networks.

Interest rates

Another much more simple but still effective strategy to time markets is to take a look at the current and future prospects for interest rates.

The Fed often lowers interest rates going into a bear market as the economy gets progressively worse and starts to raise them only when the economy has started to pick up. We saw this in early 2008 before one of the more severe bear markets of the century.

A good strategy, therefore, is to buy stocks when rates are low and are about to turn up and to sell stocks when rates are high. Many traders try to tell you the opposite, that cutting rates boosts stocks. This is true over the short-term but over the longer term, interest rate cuts actually indicate a worsening economic environment. Timing the market like this would have paid big dividends over most of the last century.

Getting the edge with open position data

As we have seen, it is market participants who ultimately drive prices through the act of buying and selling various futures – so it's fair to say that knowledge of who is buying what, and how much, would be extremely useful information for predicting and timing future price moves.

Well, the good news is that by using a few different reports it is possible to do just that.

Commitment of Traders report

The Commitment of Traders (COT) report is published by the Commodity Futures Trading Commission every Friday at around 2:30pm EST. It is the best available source for gauging what market participants are doing.

The data itself is split between three groups: Commercial traders, non-commercial traders and retail traders. Generally, the commercial traders are the big corporations and banks that use markets to hedge their exposure, while the non-commercial traders are the large speculators and fund traders. The retail traders are the small guys that make up the rest of the market.

Identifying extremes

The best way to use this data, then, is to look for market extremes, as it is at these times markets are most likely to hit a top or a bottom.

Generally, when most traders move to one side of the trade it is a clear signal that markets are reaching a peak. If everyone is long, for example, then there is no one left to buy, so in theory, markets will start to fall back. Conversely, if nearly everyone is short, then there is no one left to sell.

By looking for these moments, it is possible to find times when markets spring back, like an elastic band, and when combined with other fundamental factors, a useful strategy can be developed.

Commercial and non-commercial traders

Another thing to look out for is the fact that commercial and non-commercial traders diverge as a market's peak or trough is reached. Since commercial traders are mainly looking to hedge, they tend to buy as markets hit a bottom and sell as markets reach a top. Conversely, non-commercial traders like to follow trends, so tend to be more bearish at market bottoms and bullish at market tops.

If you see a market extreme whereby a large proportion of traders are positioned on one side of the trade and this is accompanied with divergence between the positions of commercial and non-commercial traders, this is a strong sign that a market extreme is near.

Short interest data

In stocks, one way to see what traders are doing in a particular company is to look at the short interest data. This data can be extracted from the central exchange and shows the number of shares that have been sold short in a stock divided by its daily volume.

The ratio therefore indicates the proportion of investors who are bearish on a stock and can be used to decide whether to go long or short. If a stock has a high number of short sellers, then it stands to reason that it could decline in the near future. Although if the stock has a high number of short sellers and does not move, then it could be bullish – since when bulls do join the market, stocks are likely to go up.

Short interest data can also be calculated for the entire exchange.

Oanda data

Like the COT report, there are other places where traders can find data on currency positions, such as from forex broker Oanda. The company releases details of the net long and short positions for currencies for most of its customers and lists them via its website. Although it is relatively untested, this data could be another way to gauge market sentiment. Oanda also shows data on much shorter time frames than the COT report and it is generally shown that whenever a market is over 75% net long or net short, a reversal is usually near.

HOW TO TRADE LONG-TERM TRENDS IN THE STOCK MARKET

Learning to time markets effectively is a valuable skill, it is only one component of a successful strategy.

Indeed, there are many traders who make their money fretting over the smallest daily movements but they sometimes forget to look at the bigger picture. If they only took a step back, they might realize that the major trend is perhaps more important than anything.

While timing is essential for entries and exits, it's important to concentrate on markets with the most profit potential, since the big money is saved for those investors who are able to catch the big trends and capture those 500%+ investments.

Supply and demand underpins all macro analysis

When it comes to finding long-term trends there is no substitute for doing some macro analysis into the big picture issues affecting the markets – the outlook for interest rates, for example, or the potential influence of big market players such as central banks or the International Monetary Fund. These are critical issues that have widespread implications for markets, implications that can shape markets for several years at a time.

Supply and demand is the underlying principle affecting all markets, although analyzing it accurately is a tricky task. For commodities traders, there are statistics for global supply and consumption (the Commodity Yearbook is an excellent resource for this), while seasonal variations also come into play. In bonds, demand can be measured through auctions and in stocks, the value of a business determines its demand, relative to price.

It's also useful to consider world history when assessing the current environment. Has this situation ever occurred before in the past? What happened then that could happen now and what makes this situation different to that time?

Are we headed for a period of inflation like the 1970s and '80s? If so, perhaps precious metals will soar like they did then. Or, is there a chance of war? If so, will stocks go down and oil go up? These are patterns that can be found if you spend enough time looking through the history of markets.

It's also important to consider cycles, since these are grounding principles of economics. Unemployment, recessions, economic growth – in fact, most things – tend to run in cycles. It's a similar thing with markets, so identifying current cycles makes it easier to project what might happen next. Recessions typically occur every 4-6 years – something to keep in mind when considering the current valuation of the stock market and whether to invest or wait.

Another way to get on board a long-term trend is to get into the stock market when it is distressed and extremely cheap on a valuation basis. As already suggested, the best time to invest is often when there is 'blood on the streets' and panic rules. The stock market nadir of March 2009 was one such time when seemingly no one wanted to invest, yet it set in motion a 4-year bull market.

While macro analysis and fundamental data can provide effective insight into markets, sometimes you cannot beat reading straight off of a chart. After all, we are trying to make money off of price moves not economic predictions.

It's the same reason why traders use trend lines and then developed indicators such as moving averages – now popular among technical traders and trend followers.

Anyone can draw a trend line on to a chart and say where a market is headed next but moving averages offer a calculated way to see when a market is trending. When a faster moving average crosses over a slower one, it signals that an upward trend has formed and these signals can be used to join long-term trends in any market. In this way, you can largely forget about the fundamental picture and just focus on price and making a profit.

A popular combination used by some professionals is to buy markets when the 50-day exponential moving average (EMA) crosses the 200-day EMA, known as a 'golden cross'. Buying markets on a golden cross gets you on board most long-term trends – such as the big bull market in the Dow during the '90s, for example, and the 10-year run-up in gold. You won't catch it right at the bottom or get out at the top but you can catch a big chunk of the middle, which is what good trend following is all about.

HOW TO DEVELOP YOUR OWN INDICATORS

It is important to develop your own view as to where you think markets may be headed and there are plenty of indicators out there for you to use. You can do this using fundamental indicators or technical indicators. Whatever works as a means of predicting future price moves should be judged on its own merit.

However, there is an inherent flaw in using a well-known indicator, you are likely getting the same trading signals as everyone else who uses it.

The solution of course is to develop your own indicators and it isn't as difficult as it seems.

Technical indicators

Indicators do not have to be particularly complex but they do need to make sense. The best way to approach designing a technical indicator, therefore, is to first scour several different price charts looking for patterns in the data.

By scanning lots of different situations over various time horizons, you should be able to come up with a unique idea that you think may lead to profitable trading opportunities.

Once you have an idea, it is simply a matter of getting that idea on paper in the form of programming code, since nearly anything that you can see on a price chart can be distilled down into mathematical code.

Most trading platforms allow coding and if you are not too keen on doing it yourself, you can get a programmer to do it for you.

Once you have your own personal indicator written down in code, you can start adding buy and sell arguments, and go about testing how effective it is trading on historical price data.

Fundamental indicators

Many traders forget that indicators can be designed to use fundamental data, not just price data alone.

It's possible to download economic data from many of the freely available sources on the Internet and incorporate it into your investment decisions. (Several spreadsheets of economic data have been included in the download pack that accompanies this book.)

There are plenty of options around which can be combined into a composite indicator or simply used on their own.

You could, for example, create a composite indicator that measures the spreads between bond yields and takes into account the price earnings of stocks in the S&P 500. Or one that keeps track of M3 money supplies in the economy and the price of oil.

By doing so, you could limit your account to only trade when certain fundamental conditions line up. This way, you can use fundamental data as a type of filter for your trades.

As another example, let's say that the spread between interbank rates and T-Bills is higher than 1 (also known as the TED spread, an indicator which signifies credit risk and thus fear in the market). You could use this information as a filter and only buy safe-haven assets such as gold or the Swiss franc. Similarly, if the TED spread is lower than 1, the market is more optimistic so you might choose to only buy riskier assets like stocks. (An example of this strategy is provided in the Trading Systems chapter.)

HOW TO USE MOMENTUM INVESTING TO YOUR ADVANTAGE

So far, we have spoken a little bit about trend following and the methods professionals use to find trends, so it makes sense to say a few words about momentum investing, which bears a lot of similar traits.

Although it operates on much longer time frames, momentum investing has been one of the 'darlings' of the investment world in recent years. For the last few years, fund managers using momentum techniques have consistently proclaimed returns that have beaten the S&P 500 by at least 5 percentage points on average per year. Because of this, momentum investing is regarded as one of the better investment strategies all around.

In fact, momentum investing is one of a handful of investment strategies that has been corroborated by academic research.

The basic idea behind momentum investing is to buy securities that have performed the best over the preceding 3-12 months and to sell those that have performed the worst, thus hoping to catch profitable long-term trends. By doing so, money is always invested and is simply moved around to the best performing assets.

According to the founder of momentum investing, Richard Driehaus, 'far more money is made by buying high and selling higher' than the traditional Wall Street adage of 'buy low and sell high'. It is this same principle that can be found in many trend following strategies.

Indeed, like trend following, you typically do not need to know anything about the chosen stock or security other than its previous monthly or annual return, making the strategy attractive for its simplicity and ease of use, as well as its ability to generate high returns.

Another benefit is that momentum investing can be applied to all sorts of investments, not just stocks. Bonds, commodities, ETFs and currencies all seem to work well with momentum investing –

the principle being that trends exist in all types of markets due to the nature of market cycles. By moving out of weak assets into strong assets, diversification and big profits can be achieved at the same time.

A momentum strategy, for example, would have moved into bonds and out of stocks during early 2008 and thus would have been largely immune from the stock market crash.

However, with many academics now agreeing that momentum investing has been a successful way of beating the market since as far back as the 1900s, the question of whether it will continue to be so is of paramount importance to investors.

With more traders aware of the benefits of this strategy, it could be that market inefficiencies that make the strategy work may erode, thus destroying the profitability of the system. In theory, this could be the case for any system that gains popularity.

Some analysts have recently argued that this may be just the case and that momentum investing exists because of a behavioral phenomenon, not a fundamental one, and big hedge funds harnessing the strategy are eroding the strategy's profit potential.

The fact remains, however, that big trends are a feature of the world – just look at the long bull market in bonds, and the fact that gold went up 10 years in a row. These trends are unlikely to ever go away, as they are a result of the way economic cycles operate. Momentum investing offers the investor a unique way to profit from these trends and is a method that can be used in conjunction with other strategies to offer a diversified and less risky portfolio.

Getting started with momentum investing

It is possible to set up your own momentum investing strategy through any good stockbroker. It's just a matter of moving your investments into the best performing assets over the previous time period, but you should test your strategy out first before beginning.

Alternatively, you can invest in a number of managed funds that operate using a momentum investing strategy such as the AQR Small Cap Momentum Fund (ASMOX).

Such funds usually charge an annual fee between 1-3% and may also take a share of any profits.

DOLLAR COST AVERAGING

While momentum investing is great for growing your portfolio, dollar cost averaging (DCA) is another investment strategy which offers real benefits. It is not a trading strategy but an investment approach that you can use over long-term time frames and benefits from having a regular stream of income.

Simply, DCA involves investing an equal portion of capital on an investment or portfolio over regular periods. For example, investing $1000 into the S&P 500 index each month.

Thus, the benefit of DCA is that the amount of shares that can be bought with the money will vary inversely with the price. In other words, when the price is high, you can afford fewer shares; when the price is low you can afford more. It's the same technique that many pension schemes are based on.

The end result is a general lowering of the average cost per share, which means over time you can build a portfolio that is made up of a majority of investments purchased at average lower costs.

Although DCA is not always the best strategy for lump sum invest-ing, if you have a regular stream of income DCA is probably one of the best strategies out there for increasing wealth.

It's particularly effective when used with indices or ETFs as these types of markets never go to zero – which is the only real risk when using the DCA approach.

(You can have a look at the types of returns possible with DCA in Chapter 6 where I have tested the strategy over 10 years of data.)

Getting started with DCA

Utilizing a DCA strategy can be done through any stock broker but it requires you to remember to invest in your portfolio each month and to stay disciplined during market declines.

Fortunately, there are a number of alternatives online that can manage the process for you.

CHAPTER 3:
RISK

MONEY MANAGEMENT AND TRADING PSYCHOLOGY

To understand these two subjects, is to first realize that traders operate in a constant world of risk. To make money in this game is to take on risk with the hope of reward. It is this balance that must drive every trading decision. Whenever we are in a trade we are at risk, since any price decline can lead to the loss of capital.

Although I have left this section until Chapter 3, it does not mean that these two topics are less important. In fact, nothing could be further than the truth. Good money management and a good mindset are probably the most important ingredients to successful trading. Without these, even the best traders would go broke.

Good money management

There is no right or wrong answer when it comes to managing risk. Each trader must work out what works best for them on the basis of their trading strategy and personality. There are, however, a number of things you can do to greatly improve your chances.

Fixed lots vs. fractional bets

Most professional traders trade their accounts using either fixed lots or fractional bets. Fixed lots trade a set amount for each trade (for example $10 per pip), whereas fractional bets are based on the percentage of the fund that is invested. Neither is better than the other, though fixed lot trading is probably more suited to shorter-term trading such as day trading.

Fractional trading (trading a certain percentage of an account) helps compounding and generally leads to bigger returns – though usually at the expense of bigger drawdowns.

As a general rule, it is advisable to never risk more than 1-2% of your capital on any one trade.

Just to be clear, the distance between your entry and your typical exit should not equate to more than 1-2 % of your capital.

You should trade small enough you won't go broke but large enough to make it worthwhile.

When putting money at play in markets, it is important to know exactly what you stand to lose if you are wrong and what you stand to gain if you are right. As a general rule, you should trade light enough so that the risk of going broke is extremely small but large enough to make the experience worthwhile. If it's not worthwhile you will simply become bored and complacent.

The difficulty comes because of slippage and unforeseen events, and it is impossible to calculate exactly how much capital is always at risk. However, there are a number of things we can do to estimate the risk and control it.

Stop orders

Stop orders are essential tools traders use to manage risk. By placing a stop loss order at a certain level, the amount of money that is put at risk is limited to the distance between your entry price and the stop level. For example:

Suppose you have just entered a long position in the EUR/USD currency pair at a level of 1.2950, hoping it goes up. You do not want to lose more than $500 on the trade so you place a stop loss order 50 pips away from the market at 1.2900 (since each pip is worth $10). Now, even if the market goes to 1.2800, you are protected and only lose the $500.

It is worth remembering, however, that sometimes the market may gap down below your stop level, which means it is filled at the next best price – at 1.2895, for example. This can happen in times of volatility and is called 'slippage'. It just goes to show that risk management is not an exact science. As with most things in trading, it usually pays to err on the side of caution.

Where to place your stops

For some traders, stops are essential tools for ensuring they never lose more money than they bargained for. But for other traders, stops can actually be harmful, since sometimes markets hit stops and then reverse back the other way. It is important therefore to test a trading strategy properly and work out where the best place is to put a stop.

For example, upon testing a strategy it may become clear that the system almost never makes any money after it drops 12 pips. A good stop could therefore be placed 12 pips below the market since it catches all the losing trades that never make any profit but does not cut short in duration the trades that do go on to make money.

Similarly, some systems may lose money if the stops are placed too tight. In this case, you may want to move the stop further away and have the system exit positions, using some other logic such as moving average crossovers or volatility thresholds.

The important thing is to test the strategy to find out what its characteristics are. For systems traders, the maximum adverse execution (MAE) and maximum favorable execution (MFE) metrics are excellent tools for analyzing where to place stops, as they identify where the most profitable areas are to place them.

Finding the optimal position size

Whether you use stops or not, it is important to consider carefully how much you are going to bet on each trade. It is a common mistake amongst traders to just bet a certain percentage of their fund based on how much they have available. This is generally an inefficient way to allocate your resources. In fact, if your strategy is strong you can work out what is the best-sized bet for each trade.

Let's say we have a trading system that is right 50% of the time with a risk/reward ratio of 2:1. It stands to reason that if these statistics stay the same over a large sequence, we can work out the best amount of money to bet to maximize our return.

In this case, we would bet 25% of our bankroll.

The method many professionals use to calculate this optimal position size is using an equation called the Kelly Formula, which was developed in 1956 by J. L. Kelly.

The Kelly formula

This formula uses a system's risk/reward ratio and probability of winning to give the position size that results in the fastest appreciation of the trading account. The formula is as follows:

K = W – (1 – W)/R

Where:

K = Fraction of capital for next trade

W = Historical win ratio (wins/total trials)

R = Winning payoff rate

So if a trade has a risk/reward of 2:1 with a 50-50 chance of winning, then:

K = .5 – (1 - .5)/2 = .5 - .25 = .25

The Kelly formula indicates the optimal fixed-fraction bet is 25%.

As a general rule, I have found that a lot of profitable systems have optimal position sizing in the 20-25% range. In practice, many traders then halve the Kelly formula in order to stay on the cautious side.

Diversification

Another trick traders use to improve their returns is with diversification. (I will talk about this a bit more in the next chapter.) However, simply put, if we are able to spread our risk across different markets, it is possible to improve prospective returns while reducing drawdown levels.

For example, let's say we have calculated the Kelly formula as 24%

and have divided it by 2 giving us 12%. What we can do, is split that 12% into 12 positions of 1% risk, or 6 positions of 2% risk. As long as the trading strategy is robust, we end up with the same reward but with risk spread across different positions. This leads to better returns and a smoother equity curve.

Always know what your risk is

Successful money management is a vast topic and is only briefly touched upon here. Many traders advise the 1-2% rule; splitting your investment into positions of 1-2% risk, when trading and it is fairly sound advice.

However, the truth is that no two strategies are ever the same. Successful money management requires knowing your trading strategy inside and out, and finding the amount of risk that allows the fastest appreciation of capital while guarding against drawdown. Risking too much on one trade inevitably leads to wipeout, so trade conservatively at all times. A good book on this subject is The New Money Management by Ralph Vince.

TRADING PSYCHOLOGY

Whether you are new to the markets or you are an experienced veteran you are probably aware of the huge role psychology plays in successful trading. Financial markets swell on the hopes and fears of its participants, which often leads to market moves that no one would have predicted. Indeed, you only have to make a small trade to experience the emotions of fear and greed that come with putting your money in the hands of markets.

Get to know yourself

The first thing you must do in order to conquer the psychological aspects of trading is to know what makes you tick and what your trading personality is. What is your tolerance to risk and what do you need to do to ensure you make the correct trading decisions?

If, for example, you find it hard to tolerate big intraday swings, you may wish to try swing trading instead of day trading. If you find your emotions are causing you to frequently change your mind about your trading decisions, then you should consider developing a system.

In the same way, it is always possible to improve your mindset, so think about keeping a journal detailing your trade rationale and your emotions at the time of each trade. Continually re-evaluate your diary so that you can see where you are going wrong and how you can overcome your limitations.

Positive mental attitude

Ed Seykota, one of the best traders of all time, is famous for saying 'everyone gets what they want out of the market', which basically means that if you want to lose, you will lose, and if you want to win, you will win.

It sounds ludicrous and simplistic but it's true. Seykota has touched on the fact that people often bring a lot of baggage and personal conflict to markets, which can subconsciously derail them from making the right decisions. The best traders, therefore, tend to be grounded and level-headed and have positive expectations for each trade. If you feel that you might have subconscious feelings that are conflicting against your best wishes, try to get them resolved before you think about trading.

I have never been the best at visualization, but it is generally a good idea to try and stay positive, always remind yourself why it is you are trading and remember to keep your goals in sight. Try to visualize yourself reaching those goals and keep up a positive internal dialogue as often as you can. This can be difficult at first but the more you practice it the more natural it becomes.

Also, give yourself clear rules in order to help separate your emotional self from the market and try to surround yourself with other, positive people with similar goals. There is no harm in asking a friend to monitor your positions and to instruct them to interfere if you break your rules. Similarly, you could download software that stops you from trading at certain times. It really doesn't matter what it is or what people think, if it works for you then do it.

Try to take regular exercise too, mental and physical, and make sure to give yourself a break when tired or if you just don't feel like trading. Many traders try to battle through such periods of trading fatigue and wind up giving weeks of hard earned cash back to the markets.

Overcome your emotions

One of the reasons why trading is so difficult is that it requires you to act contrary to your natural human emotions. For example, it feels much more natural to buy something when it is going up than when it is going down. However, making money in trading requires the exact opposite – that is, to buy low and sell high.

Similarly, when you are in a trade and you are losing money, the natural human response is to wait, with the hope it eventually turns around. Of course, this greed often just leads to bigger losses and the best response is often to cut your losses as soon as you can. There are similar problems when holding on to winning positions since you do not want to take profits too soon out of fear, or too late, again, out of greed.

This dichotomy between natural instinct and the psychology need-ed to beat the markets does present its own opportunity however. By becoming aware of these limitations, it is easier to find the times when markets are beset by panic, or overcome with euphoria. Mar-kets are basically one big representation of the hopes and fears of the crowd. It is at these extremes that the best trades can often be found.

Mange risk effectively

Key to overcoming your emotions also comes back to managing risk effectively which we spoke about earlier. Since money can have the biggest impact on your emotions, you must trade at a level that is comfortable enough for your own personality. Trading too big simply increases your emotional responses, meaning that making the right trading decision becomes almost impossible.

Similarly, trading too small can lead to overtrading and complacency. To manage risk successfully you need to come up with a strategy that works for you and then be consistent at implementing it. Because all it takes is one trade that is too big to completely derail your mindset.

Never stop learning

One of the great things about trading is that financial markets are continually evolving. This means that trading often becomes an all-consuming endeavor creating immense satisfaction for those who partake in it.

Every day brings new world events and possibilities for profit. It is a game of such complexity that one can never be bored. It stands to reason then, that the successful trader is one that is continually reading, learning and adapting.

To succeed, it is important to always learn about new technologies, about new events, new strategies and theories. Naturally, this also means to stay humble, since markets have a knack for destroying traders who are too arrogant for their own good.

Arrogance is the best friend of complacency, always approach the markets with an optimistic but cautious mindset. And to this end, it is important to remember the final necessity for winning at trading.

Perseverance

Indeed, the path to riches is strewn with the corpses of countless traders who tried and failed in their conquest for trading fulfillment. Successful traders come in many different forms and use many different techniques. However, there is one specific trait that all successful traders share – they never give up.

CHAPTER 4:
TRADING TIPS

TIPS & SECRETS

We have covered some of the most important aspects in trading. It's time to look at some tips that should put you in good stead for when you choose to go it alone in the markets.

HOW TO BEAT THE PROFESSIONALS AT THEIR OWN GAME

The stock market is indeed a dangerous place for beginners, which is why some investors choose the trusted advice of Wall Street professionals and advisors over their own intuition. For some, I do not doubt this is a sensible choice and worth the extra money that comes with employing a professional in the field.

However, by following a few simple rules, it is possible for the average investor to beat the professionals at their own game. I don't know about you but I would rather know what I am doing before handing over my money to anybody else.

There is no substitute for hard work

The best way to beat the pros is to do your homework and plenty of it. While professional brokers often have to split their time meeting with customers and representing their business (usually at boozy client lunches), you can get ahead by researching as much as you can.

In fact, just by reading the annual reports of the companies you are interested in, you have probably done more research than the average Wall Street professional. Take your research a step further by listening to company conference calls (freely available on most company websites these days) and scanning company balance sheets for irregularities. These can all be found easily online with websites such as Yahoo! Finance.

Focus on a niche area, invest in what you know

A Wall Street broker is often disadvantaged by the fact that they cannot always choose the sectors they are most interested in. They may be tasked by their company to research all the companies in the oil space or all the pharmaceutical companies in the mid-west for example. Strict company hierarchies mean brokers sometimes have to do jobs that they would rather not do.

You can take advantage of this by focusing on what you know. Maybe you have specialist knowledge of the auto industry or maybe you are excited about a new technology being developed by your own employer. By focusing on a niche area, which can be as small as one or two companies, you can gain a huge advantage and turn your own expertise into valuable information to play the markets with.

Look at harnessing new tools for social media

If we consider what exactly we are up against we can see that the average Wall Street professional is in their late 30s-50s, white collared, with a science or math degree from a good school. They may know a lot about biotech or Silicon Valley but there are certain areas such as popular culture where their knowledge is bound to fail.

By staying alert to the world around you, you can find investment opportunities in your everyday life that the Wall Street pros may likely miss. Products such as Apple's iPod, Crocs shoes and Nintendo's Wii were all products that took a long time for Wall Street to latch on to. Even Apple was ignored for a time before it became the most popular stock on the planet.

If you have kids, keep an ear out to what they are interested in and keep your eyes open to what products are selling like hot cakes in your local shopping mall. Tap into social media, sites like Facebook and Twitter, which allow virtually anyone to be able to track trends and new developments, and you can be on your way to finding the next big investment. Look at ways to interpret data such as with Google Analytics or Twitter APIs.

I was skeptical about such methods at first but after reading Chris Camillo's book, Laughing at Wall Street, I changed my mind. Camillo turned a few thousand dollars into over $2 million in just a couple of years using some of these methods.

Exotic investments, out of the reach of your typical broker

Once again, there are plenty of advantages to be had by trading for yourself. As an employee of a firm, most Wall Street pros are only able to invest in certain securities. Maybe they can only invest in tech stocks, for example, or maybe they are only able to invest in US listed companies, or companies over a certain market capitalization.

You are not bound by the same limitations so do your research and find the securities that the professionals cannot trade. Foreign stocks, commodities, currencies, new frontiers – there are plenty of different ways to fulfill your winning portfolio. Once you start doing your research and poring over stock charts, the ideas will come flooding in.

DIVERSIFICATION...AGAIN

We briefly touch upon diversification in the previous chapter and go into it in a bit more detail here, because it really is another pro secret that is going to help you beat the markets.

In fact, diversification is called 'the only free lunch' in the investment world, because it is an easy and inexpensive way to guard a portfolio against inherent market risks while giving you the opportunity to increase your profits.

When people talk about diversification, they often say, 'don't put all your eggs in one basket' or something similar. While this is accurate and a useful reminder, the problem is that it does not allow investors to think more smartly about where to put their 'eggs'. The truth is, there are countless ways to diversify a portfolio. It all depends on the contents of the portfolio and your preference for risk.

The golden rule to remember is that effective diversification is based on correlation. The lower the correlation between securities, the better diversified the portfolio.

Bonds

As I referred in Chapter 1, bonds are probably the most popular investments to diversify a portfolio with, since they generally move in the opposite direction of stocks. They are true safe-haven investments, so having some exposure to bonds means that when your stocks go down the value of your bonds are likely to go up.

Of course this is not always the case, as inefficiencies in markets can cause even negatively correlated investments to move in the same direction at times, so you still need to do your homework. Bonds come in different forms too. Government bonds are generally safer than corporate bonds (depending on the government). Bonds move in the opposite way to interest rates, so you should also have a view about inflation.

Gold

Another popular tool used to diversify portfolios is gold, as it acts not only as a hedge against inflation but as a safe-haven investment as well.

Since the metal is priced in US dollars, it guards against depreciation in the dollar meaning it retains value as everything else inflates. If your portfolio is largely made up of US stocks, it is important to protect the dollar value of your investments; owning gold is one of the best ways to do that. Because of its inherent rarity, gold also acts as a safe haven and is a solid addition to a long-term portfolio.

Foreign currencies

Just as gold can protect a dollar-denominated portfolio, so too can foreign currencies. By owning a portion of euros, British pounds,

Swedish krones, or better yet all three, your dollar-denominated portfolio is diversified and better equipped to deal with fluctuations in currency markets.

Once again, you can improve your chances by doing some research into which currencies you think may improve over time.

It's important not to diversify for the sake of it but to try and improve your returns. So take a look at the future prospects for countries around the world. If you believe New Zealand will be a force to be reckoned with in a few years' time, then take a look at buying some New Zealand dollars. Likewise, if you think the Japanese yen is undervalued, buy some of those.

Other sectors

The truth is, there are countless ways to diversify a portfolio. If you like tech stocks and have bought Apple but dislike financials, you could diversify by shorting Citigroup (financial services) – but only if you believe doing so benefits both trades.

Or, if you have bought into oil stocks, you could diversify by buying pharmaceutical stocks or discretionary stocks. The correlation between the two is not negative, but you achieve some level of diversification that can help offset losses. Try and find markets that are different but also likely to go up together. There are thousands of possibilities.

Foreign shares

Just as gold and foreign currencies offer hedges, foreign stocks give good diversification to a portfolio by exposing it to new areas. These days, it has never been easier to invest in foreign shares, as the proliferation of American Depository Receipts (ADRs) means many foreign stocks are listed on US exchanges.

While it is also possible to invest in foreign stocks directly (and this can be done through most online brokers now), trading ADRs means there is no need for any currency conversion.

Similarly, many big US-based companies have strong exposure to foreign areas such as China, so buying into these can be a good diversifier if you know enough about the company and its prospects. Intel, for example, derives around 50% of its revenue from China. So it isn't just exposure to the US that you are getting when you invest.

However, you must temper that with an understanding of currency markets and whether the companies are involved in imports or exports. They are the ones most affected by changes in foreign exchange.

Generally, a depreciating currency is good news for a company (or country) that is a big exporter, while a strengthening currency is better for importers – since more products can be imported at the same nominal cost.

You must also consider foreign exchange risk when you buy a foreign stock, since you are effectively also buying foreign currency. Buying a foreign stock that goes up 10% is no good if the value of its native currency drops 10%.

One way to negate this is to use currency futures to hedge your currency risk or you could look for stocks that can benefit from your expected currency moves.

Indices and exchange traded funds

Stock market indices and bonds can be used for diversification purposes because they are an easy way to gain exposure to an area with which you are not currently invested. Likewise with exchange traded funds (ETFs) – they track several different investments at once and exhibit a smoothing effect, meaning they can be less volatile. Essentially then, ETFs and indices are already diversified investments to a certain extent.

Combinations

If you are big on large caps you could buy a small caps index. If you have a lot of gold stocks in your portfolio, you could buy USD or buy an oil ETF or an ETF linked to the Chinese stock market. The list is endless. But remember, the smaller the correlation between markets the greater the diversification, and correlation between different assets changes over time.

Above all, make sure not to diversify just for the sake of it. Because there comes moments when diversification, like other trading techniques, flies out the window.

Sometimes, like during big market crashes, many securities end up all moving in the same direction – down. Just look at 2008, when gold, commodities and stocks all crashed at once. In this case, diversification would have helped but it would have been no substitute for solid risk control.

There are plenty of ways to diversify, but ultimately each investment should confirm your overall world view. Be creative and think of ways to spread your risk and increase your profits at the same time.

THE MAGIC OF COMPOUNDING

While diversification is referred to as 'the only free lunch' in the investment world, traders often quote the effect of compounding as being the eighth wonder of the world. It's seemingly magical ability to turn small amounts of money into vast fortunes has been harnessed to great affect by some of the world's best traders. It is a secret you would be foolish to ignore.

We saw in the last chapter, two different techniques of using money management in markets and showed that fractional bets can be an effective way of growing wealth. Investing a percentage of your capital instead of a fixed sum allows the magic of compounding to take place and enables a more optimal bet size to be placed. The best way to see this is to look at an example:

Let's say that Trader A saves $25,000 of his salary per year while

Trader B starts off with just $1 and doubles it each year. Under this scenario, it would take Trader A 40 years investing half of his salary to become a millionaire, meanwhile Trader B has invested just $1 and has reached a million in just 20 years.

Doubling your money every year like this may not be realistic, however the principle of compounding remains the same – the sooner you start, the sooner you benefit.

As another example, let's say Trader B starts investing at age 24 and puts $2,000 a year into the market for the next six years, in a portfolio that returns 12%. Meanwhile Trader A waits until 30 before also investing $2,000 per year and invests the same amount each year until the age of 65.

By retirement then, Trader A and Trader B are both millionaires, however, Trader B has invested just $12,000, over six years, while Trader A has invested $72,000 over 36 years. As you can see, the effects of compounding increases with time and the sooner you can put your money to work the better.

Formula for compounding:

$FV = P(1 + i)n$

Where:

FV = future value amount including the principal

P = principal amount

i = rate of interest per year

n = number of years invested

In order to fully benefit from compounding you therefore need to invest at the highest level of interest for the longest period of time. A portfolio that returns just 3% a year turns a sum of $10,000 into just $18,000 after 20 years. While a portfolio that returns 20% per year turns the same amount into nearly $400,000.

It therefore makes sense to aim for high-yielding investments if you can – especially while young – in the hope that they balance out over time.

THE EFFECT OF NEWS RELEASES ON THE MARKETS

As the saying goes, 'there is more than one way to skin a cat,' this is true for trading too, where there is more than one way to make a living. While some traders rely on fundamental analysis and others on their technical skills, some are able to make a good living trading news events and economic releases alone.

To trade the news effectively, traders need access to quick connections since economic events and news releases have the power to move markets in a matter of seconds. It's therefore useful to fork out a bit of money for reliable data sources and news feeds.

However, many news releases come out and have little to no effect on markets whatsoever. It's imperative to know which news releases have the most potential to move markets.

The popularity of certain news items tends to come and go, and while it is true that news events have different effects depending upon the phases of markets, these are the biggest movers at the present time:

US non-farm payrolls

Non-farm payrolls (NFP) tend to be the most watched event in the trading calendar. The number is released on the first Friday of each month at 13:30 GMT (unless the Friday falls on a public holiday). The figure is a read of current unemployment in the States and is a good indicator of the strength of the economy. The payrolls number always brings significant volatility to markets with an average pip movement of around 150 pips in USD after the number is released. The release has a similar effect on stocks and other asset classes.

Central bank announcements

Central banks can cause major movements in markets and this is especially true in bonds, stocks and currencies. Interest rate hikes or cuts have the power to really disrupt markets especially if the decision is a surprise. Although volatility for central bank decisions comes and goes, traders sometimes attribute more importance to them than anything else.

For example, markets are currently very worried about Fed tapering, and thus pay a lot of attention to what the Fed's Chair, Ben Bernanke, has to say.

US retail sales, trade balance and CPI

US retail sales come out as the second biggest market moving news release after non-farm payrolls, with an average movement of around 80 pips in USD after the release. Similarly, the US trade balance number typically moves the dollar by around 70 pips and the consumer price index (CPI) by about 60 pips. The CPI figure typically becomes more or less important depending on whether markets are concerned with inflation or deflation. There is similar volatility in the main stock indices and commodity markets.

Trading these news releases is pretty straightforward once you know how. There are plenty of economic calendars available on the Internet that detail all the big releases for the coming week and their predicted outcomes.

Other events

Of course, traders need to also be able to react to big news events such as outbreaks of war or natural disasters. These disaster-type scenarios typically lead traders into safe havens such as bonds, the Swiss franc, US dollar or gold.

HOW TO TRADE NON-FARM PAYROLLS

As we have just seen, for the news trader, there is possibly no other more important number than the monthly NFP report. It is this number that paints the clearest picture of the current state of the US economy. Although unemployment can be a lagging indicator, the NFP report is still a key consideration when central banks decide on their monetary policies.

In fact, the Fed has recently stated that its current mandate is to reduce levels of quantitative easing only when unemployment has dropped below the 6.5% mark. So you can see how important this number is, when its result can spur the world's biggest central bank into action.

Interpreting the non-farm payrolls number

As noted above, the NFP number is always released at 13:30 GMT, on the first Friday of the month, and is released alongside the underlying unemployment level. To interpret the number is straight-forward.

The headline number of payrolls indicates the number of jobs added in the US economy (minus agricultural jobs) and the underlying rate simply explains the total percentage of the population considered unemployed.

Trading the number

The most obvious way to trade the release would be to buy stocks when payrolls come in higher than expected and sell when they come in lower than expected, since more unemployment indicates a weakening economy and vice versa. (Any trading calendar on the Net is able to tell you the previous NFP number and the current months expected figure, based on analyst predictions).

However, markets are never so predictable and there are a lot of different factors that affect how markets react to the release. It all depends on market sentiment and what traders are expecting.

Lately, for example, markets have been rallying (going higher) off of a poor NFP number, since a poor figure intensifies pressure on the Fed to maintain quantitative easing which is good for stocks.

The approach strategy

To overcome this problem, some traders use what is known as an approach strategy, where they form an opinion on market sentiment and place a trade in the predicted direction as the news release approaches.

It is possible to judge sentiment successfully by looking at recent news releases. If markets respond positively to a good number, then market sentiment is bullish. However, if markets do not respond much to a good number, this is a sign that market sentiment is bearish.

If done successfully, you can judge sentiment correctly and have a small profit before the news release comes out. You can then move your stop up to break even and limit losses. Then, when the report comes out and markets move, the trade either stops out for no loss or is in a decent sized profit. Effectively, a free trade.

A good example of this occurred many times during the financial crisis when markets were forever in fear of a bad payrolls number. Such a number could cause stocks to plummet and, because of this, no one carried a long position going into the figure. Stocks nearly always began to slide just an hour or two before the release. Then, when the figure came out, markets dropped sharply, giving huge profits to those who were short.

Shorting or buying markets an hour or so before a release, then bringing down a stop loss to your entry point, is an excellent strategy for NFPs. This works on other big news releases too, particularly central bank announcements. In fact, I used this strategy a number of times for payrolls and interest rate announcements and was able to capture 100 or so pips in just a few minutes trading the indices.

While the approach strategy works well for big news events such as NFP, it is essential to know what markets are expecting. Only by judging market sentiment successfully can you attempt to predict how it will react.

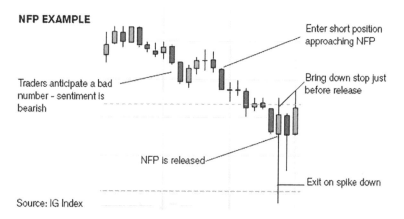

NFP EXAMPLE

Enter short position approaching NFP

Traders anticipate a bad number - sentiment is bearish

Bring down stop just before release

NFP is released

Exit on spike down

Source: IG Index

HOW TO BUY THE RUMOR, SELL THE FACT

'Buy the rumor, and sell the fact,' is a phrase that is often bandied around finance channels like the Wall Street Journal and CNBC. It describes how markets are able to react to future events before they take place.

But explaining how to buy the rumor, sell the fact, relies first on understanding a key point about how financial markets operate.

That is, that markets at any one point in time, represent all the information that is available to participants. In other words, everything that can be known about markets in the public sphere is already priced in.

Rumor, or market sentiment, is therefore a kind of information which is also priced into the markets – and by pricing in, I mean that market prices already reflect this information and the chances of it happening.

Rumor, therefore, should be given just as much importance as factual information, since it can move markets in just the same way.

Let's say, for example, the sentiment among traders is that the Fed is to begin tapering off quantitative easing at their next meeting. Bloomberg analysts rate this chance as 65%, but this is based solely on analyst opinion and no concrete fact. In other words, the rumour is that the Fed indeed tapers in the upcoming meeting.

Now, since the market fully knows about this 'rumor', it has already started to react to the upcoming event (see the spike in US Treasury yields prior to the event and the sliding off of US stocks).

The interesting thing is that markets can fully discount for the event before the event actually takes place. This means that by the time the Fed cuts quantitative easing, raises interest rates, or whatever, this news has already been priced in, and so markets may not actually react at all. This reaction has already happened running up to the event.

In fact, often the opposite is true and markets go the opposite way to what would be expected. This is especially true when the outcome is a surprise to market sentiment.

In relation to our example, let's say that the Fed do taper at the next meeting. In this situation it is unlikely there will be much of a reaction. Yet if the Fed surprises markets and does not taper, then stocks will likely rise and US Treasury yields will fall.

Hence why there can often be a lot of value in 'buying the rumor, selling the fact' or in effect, going against market sentiment.

ANOTHER APPROACH TO TRADING THE NEWS

Using sentiment to gauge the likely direction of a market during a news release, and placing a trade in that direction as the report draws near, is one good way of trading a news release when you have an idea how a market is going to move.

However, another method (one that requires no bias at all as to the likely direction), is to use a straddle strategy, whereby you place two orders either side of the market just before the release is announced.

The principle behind this strategy is that news releases often spike up or down strongly on a figure, giving enough volatility to profit from whichever direction a market takes. It's for this reason that the straddle strategy works best on the most volatile news releases – central bank announcements, non-farm payrolls and retail sales especially.

The straddle strategy

Let's say, you are a GBP/USD trader and it is the first Friday of the month. Therefore, at 13:30 GMT, the non-farm payrolls number is released – a figure that we know causes significant volatility in forex markets with an average pip movement of around 100 pips.

To use the straddle strategy then, watch how GBP/USD trades over the 30 minutes before the announcement takes place. The highest and lowest prices during this time act as your range. Just before the announcement, place two orders – the first, a sell order (a couple of pips below the bottom of your range), and the second, a buy order (a couple of pips above the top of your range).

When the news release comes out, the most likely scenario is markets spike up or down, taking out one of your orders and moving into a decent profit. You then have to make a quick decision as to whether to take the profit or hold out for a bit more. If you decide to hold out for a bit more, one option is to bring your stop down to lock in some profits.

Generally, you shouldn't try to gain much more than half of the average pip movement associated with the release. So in this case, be conservative and aim for around 40-50 pips.

Whipsaw

On occasion, it is inevitable that you will get whipsawed using the straddle strategy.

In other words, markets may move, taking out your first order before reversing and taking out your second order, in effect cancelling your position for a loss. This is inevitable and occurs when traders react to one element of a news release before realizing there is more to the data than meets the eye.

For example, non-farm payrolls are often released by the government with revisions to the previous month's number. This number has been known to affect markets when it is radically different from what was previously reported.

However, there are two solutions to this problem. The first involves initiating a third order so that when your position is cancelled, it is then also reversed at the same time. That way, you are back with a position in the direction of the markets. Depending on the volatility of the news release, doing so usually still results in a decent profit.

The second, is to pay careful analysis to the news report itself. If you are able to analyze the information quickly enough, you can make a decision to close or open your trade depending on the figure. For example, if the news release is in-line with expectations, the chances are markets may not move much. At which point, you could decide to simply close all orders and positions.

THE SHARING COMMUNITY AND TRADING WITH SOCIAL NETWORKS

I spoke briefly about the role of social media in trading, now let's elaborate on it further, since it is a growing trend amongst modern traders.

Indeed, the Internet has changed the way many industries operate; trading is no different.

Up until now, traders would historically base their trading decisions on either fundamental data or technical analysis. However, traders are increasingly looking to social networks and Web 2.0 applications to gather the information they need to trade effectively.

Facebook, and increasingly Twitter, can both be harnessed to provide insights into the masses and, thereby, indicate the future direction of markets.

There are also several new trading platforms that allow traders to follow other traders, in theory shortening the learning curve that is required to trade successfully. Many of these platforms are mostly designed for trading forex, however, they will likely be rolled out to other markets soon.

Facebook and Twitter

While Facebook and Twitter cannot be directly used to trade, they are useful tools for monitoring the crowd. Facebook can be used to track new trends and find products or events that are going viral.

Twitter especially allows traders to be able to follow trends in markets and also allows traders to follow their favorite experts, thereby receiving updates whenever that expert makes a trade.

Twitter is also an excellent resource for receiving up-to-date, breaking news stories. In fact, recent studies have shown that news is reported earlier on Twitter than any other means, including newspaper websites and company blogs.

If you can't afford an expensive news feed connection, then Twitter may be able to save you a lot of money.

ZuluTrade

To really engage in social trading, however, you may like to take a look at ZuluTrade. ZuluTrade is both one of the biggest and longest running social trading networks. It is also a place where traders come together to trade the forex markets. The service offers full trade copying of other users, supports multiple brokers and comes with a free demonstation. The basic premise of ZuluTrade is that you can search for expert traders (based on your specified metrics), and then instruct ZuluTrade to copy their trades exactly. Conversely, if you are a good trader, you can get compensated for sharing your trading signals with other users. (You'll find a more detailed review of ZuluTrade in the final chapter of this book.)

Tradency

Tradency is another platform for social trading and the company has developed a 'mirror trading' concept which allows traders to mirror the trades of selected strategies from developers around the world. The program also allows real time analysis of each trading signal which means that a trader can select trades manually too.

Personally, I am not sure about the success of some of these strategies and remain sceptical about copying other people's trades. However, new technology such as this does deserve further investigation and recognition for what it is.

MetaTrader

MetaTrader is another very popular platform with over 600 brokers and banks using the program. There are plenty of trading platforms out there but not many of them are as popular as MetaTrader.

What this means is, MetaTrader allows its huge community of traders and coders (and since 2013, all of its users) to share their own trading signals. There are now hundreds of so-called expert advisors (automated trading systems) available which can be downloaded, back-tested on historical data and then implemented through MetaTrader. For a full explanation on what an expert advisor is see the final chapter.

I am sure there are other ways to apply social media and there is sure to be more progress made on how we trade and interact with each other. As a trader, it is important to stay abreast of any developments and embrace changes. Since in the fast moving world of finance, if you don't, you are likely to be left behind.

SAFE HAVENS FOR YOUR MONEY

Social platforms may be the next big thing, but ultimately they do not help you trade unless you know more about the essentials.

We have spoken about diversification and the importance of spreading risk across different assets. However, there comes a time when even diversification is not enough and in uncertain times you may need to seek out the very safest places to put your money.

Indeed, the stock market during the last 10-12 years has been a difficult, and at times, a scary place to be with every chance it could get even worse ahead – what with many of the largest nations facing huge levels of debt and the world economy still moving sluggishly.

US treasuries as the ultimate safe haven

If you are unconcerned with capital growth, US treasuries offer the ultimate safe-haven play. The US may have lost its AAA rating but it is still one of the safest place to put your money. It would take a truly catastrophic event to bankrupt the US government to the point that it would not be able to pay back its bond holders. Since the world relies on US debt to such a massive extent, such a scenario could shatter the whole global financial system. That does not mean they are a good investment, in fact the present interest rate outlook makes them a pretty bad one. However in times of severe stress, Treasuries are still seen as one of the safest places to be.

Foreign government bonds growing in strength

Rating agencies offer a good rule of thumb when comparing the safety of bonds issued by foreign countries. But care must still be taken when investing large amounts of money, since they can sometimes be a bit slow off the ground in adjusting their valuations.

Countries such as Germany, Japan, Canada, New Zealand and China offer some of the best places to store your money if safety is what you are after. All of these countries have sound finances and growing economies, particularly China, which also has a public savings rate that is streets ahead of the rest of the world.

Precious metals for inflationary environments

Precious metals such as gold, silver and platinum are great stores of money, especially during inflationary times or economic hardship. Take a look at markets in the 1970s and ask yourself whether we can go through the same kind of scenario now.

They are real assets that are high in demand and low in supply and, due to their inherent rarity, this is unlikely to change. Make no mistake, when hard times hit and inflation ramps up to new levels, precious metals are the first to benefit as investors flock to find something that can keep their money safe.

The US dollar, the best of a bad bunch?

As the biggest economy, the US dollar retains its place as the world's global currency and is given safe-haven status by most of the world's investment community. There is no doubt this is true right now. If the problems in Europe reach a new head, investors will no doubt buy the US dollar again. But such plays are becoming increasingly short-lived and if inflation picks up, the US dollar may lose its ability to be a safe-haven play over the longer term. Currently, it exists as very much the best of a bad bunch but as inflation takes hold, currencies such as the Chinese remnimbi or the Canadian dollar may end up being safer investments after all.

Land and property

Property and land will always be in demand, as long as people want roofs over their heads and secure places to live. Land will forever be scarce so property is a relatively safe place to put your money in, and historically, returns of around 3-6% per year offer good value. The downside is property can be hard to liquidate when hard times hit. But in the meantime, at least you have somewhere to live.

Bank savings

Depending on the quality of the bank and the environment within which it operates, savings accounts in banks can be one of the safest places for your money. It pays to look around to find the best rates of interest and to investigate the investment rating provided by one of the rating agencies. In the unlikely event of a bank default, you are likely to lose money over a certain limit, therefore it pays to spread your money over a large number of different banks or investments. At the moment, the Federal Deposit Insurance Corporation (FDIC) guarantee deposits up to $50,000.

These can be classified as some of the 'safer' investments out there but it is important to realize that in the investment world nothing is ever completely safe. Furthermore, just because they are safer does not mean they are better investments. Some of these offer protection during times of stress but some, like US treasuries, may not offer particularly good long-term results. Safe-haven investments should therefore always align with your overall macro world view.

HOW TO AVOID BLOWING UP IN THE STOCK MARKET

The person you most have to fear in trading is yourself. You can be your own worst enemy when trading if you don't have dedication and a willingness to learn. Nothing can be as expensive as learning to play the stock market when you don't know what you are doing.

Here are some of the mistakes that I made when I first started and some of the common reasons why beginner traders usually lose at the first attempt. Try and avoid them at all costs.

Never trade blind

This first one seems like a no-brainer but you would be surprised at the number of people who try to play the stock market each year without having the sense to learn a thing about it.

When I first started, I thought the best strategy would be to just jump in and learn by doing. But with investing this is a flawed strategy. The stock market can be a harsh mistress and punishes those without a good system. There are few professions that are as expensive to learn as trading, so before you begin, equip yourself with the best tools, the best knowledge and the best techniques.

Similarly, never blindly follow advice or a tip from someone else. Your neighbor may truly believe that Texas Instruments is about to triple next week but if you haven't done your own research it's unlikely you have the confidence to sit with the trade once you have put it on.

Never trade by emotion

We have all experienced the emotions of greed, fear or hope. These emotions rule in the stock market even today. A piece of advice – when it comes to playing markets, the best time to buy is when people are fearful and to sell when others are greedy. It is a good, timeless piece of advice, because it goes against human nature and works more times than not.

Indeed, if you often change your position as soon as you have put it on, or sometimes do not have the courage to put on a position (instead, waiting until it is too late), then you are probably trading out of fear. Systems can be an excellent way of combating these problems.

When I first started, I only had to put on a small position before I began to feel agitated and doubtful of my choices. So much so, that today I use a much more systematic approach, which is automated by up to 80%.

Similarly, if you often add to winning positions hoping to win even more, or jump in the market at any opportunity, you are probably trading with greed.

Don't worry, it's only human and we have all been there. Do your best to conquer these emotions and you can be well on your way to trading profitably.

Never invest all your capital into one thing

This one seems like common sense too but is something I was guilty of back in the beginning.

If the last few years have taught us anything, it's that even so-called safe investments, like savings accounts, are not always completely secure. If that can be said about a bank, think about how unsafe it is to put all your money on a short-term trade.

Investments should be spread over a portfolio of different securities, so if one fails you do not lose all your money. Diversification could include bonds, currencies, precious metals, short positions or simply different stocks. If you are into shorter-term trading or investing, a good rule of thumb is to invest less than 2% per investment with an exposure of no more than 25% of your capital.

Also, you should never trade with money you can't afford to lose. You are likely to make all sorts of bad decisions and put your credit rating under threat.

Never overtrade

Investing all your money into one thing can also be called overtrading. It's risking too much capital on any one position and, quite simply, it means that one bad trade can result in losses big enough to wipe out an entire account.

The second definition of overtrading is jumping in and out of the market too many times in an attempt to catch lots of short-term moves or because you are undecided.

The problem is that the commissions for each trade significantly eat into profits and destroy your chances. Trading is not a zero sum game, because each time you trade you are paying the spread to your broker. If you make too many trades, you are effectively gambling and the commissions will destroy you.

Again, I was guilty of this problem at the beginning, largely because I didn't really know what I was doing. Once you develop a strategy that you feel confident with, the problems of overtrading tend to disappear.

Never follow tips

While it can be good practice to listen to what the experts are saying about markets it is generally not such a good idea to trade like them.

The problem with following someone else's advice is that when the trade turns sour you most likely won't have the confidence to stay in the trade. Successful traders rely on their own research and strategies that are aligned with their own risk appetite. That way, they always hold themselves responsible for taking trades and this fosters a much healthier attitude towards trading.

Another reason for not listening to someone else's trading picks is that they rarely give you all the information. The tipster may well have hedged his bet with some other trade, or they may have a take-profit target that they haven't disclosed.

Even worse, they may have a conflict of interest, such as a broker who wants you to buy a certain stock so that they receive commission for the sale.

In general, brokers are salesmen and are not the best people to listen to when making trading calls. If they were any good at trading they would probably be running hedge funds and not working as brokers.

Never place stops randomly

Markets can go in any direction, so without stops the possible downside to your investment can be limitless. That's why many successful traders use stops in the market to limit the possible downside to their investments. Many traders find that stops need to be kept super tight in order to manage risk effectively.

However, other traders find that stops can destroy their strategies if they are placed too close to the action. They therefore place their stops far away and use other rationale to exit their trades.

The best solution is to test your strategy to find out where the best place to put your stops is and to never enter them into markets randomly.

Never fight the trend

All good traders know the best way to trade in markets is to follow trends. Going against the tide can sometimes offer big rewards but it requires patience and, more often than not, it is a losing strategy in the long run. Indeed, if you look through history, most successful traders have been those who have gone with the trend. The best advice is therefore to ride winners and cut losers quickly.

Traders who try to go against the trend usually end up running out of money pretty quickly. Victor Niederhoffer is one example of a great trader who went against the trend, but even Niederhoffer ultimately experienced more than one period of bankruptcy in his career.

Never trade without a plan

It can take a bit more work but to trade the markets successfully it is vitally important to have a plan of action in place, so you know exactly what to do when things go wrong (or right). Each trade should have at the very least an entry and exit target, a stop loss point and a good reason for making the trade in the first place.

It's important to look at the current situation and imagine what would happen if markets were to change. What would happen to your investment if war broke out or the Fed raised interest rates? What would happen if oil went to $150 a barrel? Understand what could happen to your investments under different scenarios and plan what you would do when those scenarios play out.

Never trade the unknown

Many traders and investors are successful, not because they have some innate ability to time markets, but because they specialize in one or two areas and learn them inside and out. Indeed, there is no shame in concentrating on your area of interest, you don't always need to be able to trade every market under the sun.

Be it oil, gas, real estate, gold miners or biotechs, focusing on one or two areas is one of the best ways to prosper. Concentrate on what you know and you can have an edge over 99% of the rest of the markets, which in reality is all you need.

Never ignore money management

Money management is the key to successful investing. Period. In fact, excellent money management can be the difference between a profitable and a losing strategy.

I have already stated earlier in this book, as a rule of thumb, you should aim to commit only 1-2% of capital on any one trade.

Never gamble

Trading is not the same as playing roulette or blackjack. It is possible to make big money but only if you take a professional and disciplined approach at all times.

That means treating it as a full-time job and never chasing profits, never overtrading or risking it all on one trade. Trading on the basis of a whim or an emotion is akin to gambling and only ends up losing you money in the long run. Always remember, trading is not strictly a zero sum game – due to the commissions you pay every time you trade. So make sure you don't fall into the trap of trading for fun. It's a good idea to set up a separate bank account for your trading ventures and treat it as a business.

Study your performance

It seems like a no-brainer but the majority of traders are too lazy to do this one. Simply, if you want to improve your trading, it is essential to study your performance. Keep track of your performance objectively by keeping a diary or spreadsheet of every trade you make, including such things as stop loss levels and charts if necessary.

If all that sounds like too much hard work, contact your broker and have them send over your monthly statements for analysis. Once you have your 'real' stats in front of you, you can then set about seeing which areas you do well in and which ones need work.

Maybe you set your stops too tight, or maybe you become too fearful ahead of news releases. Work on those weaknesses and you can come out ahead of the traders out there who fail to learn from their mistakes.

Back-test/paper trade

One possible way to succeed in trading is to try and automate as much of the trading process as you can. That way, you automatically rid yourself of having to deal with the common pitfalls of emotional-based trading, such as fear or greed.

Furthermore, if you are able to come up with a strategy with fixed rules and objective goals, you can back-test the idea on historical data and see what would have happened if you had put the system into action. This way, you can test hundreds of different trading ideas without having to lose a penny. Similarly, it is essential to trade your strategy on paper first, before you put any real money at stake. If you can't make money paper trading, then you certainly won't be able to succeed when it's real money.

Have enough capital

Too many traders make the mistake of entering markets undercapitalized, which puts them at a disadvantage at the very start. Due to the volatility and inherent risk involved in trading, it is important to trade small, especially when you are just getting started and that means having an account big enough for you to do so.

Most traders recommend putting only 1-2% of trading capital at risk on any one trade. It is sound advice, since there are always opportunities and if you trade conservatively enough, even if you lose money, you still live to fight another day.

Choose your broker wisely

There are lots of brokers out there and some are better than others. It is, therefore, imperative to seek out a broker that is honest, reliable and one that best suits your needs. If you are a scalper, you may need an electronic communications network (ECN) broker with ultra-tight spreads. Or, if the spread does not affect your margins as much, you may want to go for a broker that excels in other areas such as in back-testing or MetaTrader compatibility. Most brokers provide demos now, so you can try out their services for free.

Learn all you can

It stands to reason that the world's wealthiest traders did not get there through luck alone. They got there by learning and studying the craft over many years and they have also studied themselves.

So always do your homework; read the best books, the best blogs and try as many things as you can to improve yourself and your trading skill.

Learn about fundamentals, interest rate differentials, the world economies, technical indicators, trading systems, price action and, most importantly, learn about sound money management. The cost of successful trading is not just the financial capital you put at risk but the time and effort that goes into perfecting the art.

Don't lose heart

Although it is painful and you should do everything you can to avoid it, if you do happen to blow your account on your first attempt, consider it as an education and do not beat yourself up over it. Many of the best traders in the world have blown up several times in their careers so don't lose heart. Take a look through the book, Market Wizards by Jack Schwager, and you realize that one or two blow-ups is actually the norm, rather than the exception for most traders. The most important thing is to learn from the process and come out as a better trader. It's much better to blow your account early on in your trading career than later on when you are managing millions of dollars.

SOME MORE TRADING SECRETS

I hope by now you are getting a feel for what it takes to be successful in the markets. Whatever anyone says, the world of finance can be an immensely difficult place to make a living, even for those who are not new to the game, so it is important to be able to access the real truth in order to succeed.

But the learning is not over yet and there are some more secrets I'd like to share with you.

These are all things that I have learned by studying practically every trading book under the sun, not to mention the valuable experience I have gained through thousands of hours of live trading.

Volume often shows direction

Volume, or the number of shares traded on a given day, is often used by traders to ascertain the real strength of a stock's price movement.

Smart traders know that if a stock jumps up on very light volume, the move is likely to be weak and could just be a technical reaction or the result of a relatively small number of players buying into the stock. Conversely, if a stock jumps up on heavy volume, it is a sure sign that the upward move has a real chance of carrying on the upward trend.

Typically, to be classed as a strong signal, volume must be at least twice as large as the recent average. So a good idea is to set up a moving average over your volume indicator on a chart. That way, you can easily see when volume has spiked over the recent norm.

Also, be aware that at certain times of the year volume drops off which can affect how markets trade. July and August are always quiet months for stock markets as many traders go on holiday, so these are generally not good months to look for big moves in the markets. In fact, some days in August you can see markets tick up for no apparent reason other than the fact that most of the big traders are not at their desks.

Other seasonal variations

A quiet August market is not the only seasonal variation that can be found in the stock market. To the untrained observer, it would seem foolish to base investment decisions on the turnings of the seasons, but there are some real patterns that professional traders use to their advantage.

'Sell in May and go away,' is one such pattern that has worked handsomely on stocks over the past few years. Since a lot of hedge funds and banks know about this pattern, it tends to pan out more than you would expect.

December is another good month for markets with the period over Christmas being especially good. So much so, that traders refer to the period between December 23 and January 1 as the Santa Claus Rally. Markets tend to tick upwards at the end of December as a result of quiet volume and investors anticipating the shifting of positions in the new year.

Indeed, early January tends to be good for markets too. It is when many big pension funds and investment vehicles adjust their portfolios for the coming year.

October is often touted as being a bad month for markets although there is a little more to it. It's true that many of the biggest market crashes have occurred in October but interestingly, on average the month has performed fairly favorably over time.

Rollovers

Another thing to look out for in your trading diary are the rollover dates for options and futures contracts. These typically occur every three months and are overlooked by most retail traders, which is unfortunate because they often provide volatility and some great trading opportunities.

As I explained at the beginning of the book, futures are settled at a point in the future depending on which contract month you have bought into.

As the end of a futures contract draws near, brokers and traders who want to rollover their trades need to close their positions and re-open them in the next month's futures contract. That way, they don't get caught holding a position prior to delivery. This often creates a good level of volatility as traders scramble to open and close their biggest positions – a good event to watch out for.

Markets do not always trend

It is a common misconception amongst some traders that markets are always in a trend and the key to making profits is to find the trend and ride it to its conclusion. However, professionals realize that markets actually spend most of the time (around 60-65%) trading in a range. Professionals know it is imperative, therefore, to have a strategy that keeps them in the money even while markets are not trending. That could be a mean reversion strategy or even just having some money on the sidelines. Alternatively, agile traders scan the gamut of world markets in order to find those markets that are trending.

Markets follow the US's lead

As the largest economic power in the world, the US has been the biggest influencer over markets for a while now and there is no evidence that this is about to change any time soon despite theories of decoupling. What this means for traders is that foreign markets nearly always follow the US's lead. 9 times out of 10, if US stock markets close higher, Asian markets will open higher too and this will very often flow through to the European session too.

Avoid stops at '00' levels

As already discussed, stop losses can be useful for guarding against adverse price moves and managing risk, but they can also lead to losing trades if they are not placed in the right area. Many newbie traders make the mistake of placing stops at key support and resistance levels (or '00' levels) like 100 or 1500. The problem is that markets nearly always hit these 'round' price levels before reversing and going back the other way.

Some traders are even suspicious and believe that brokers and floor traders can actually see where the stops are, causing them to bid markets up to those levels.

While that may have happened in the past, it is not likely to occur anymore. Still, if you are suspicious, the best solution is to use mental stops and close your trades manually once they hit your intended levels.

Shorting stocks requires extra care

Being able to short stocks means traders can profit from a fall in stock price which is essential in order to find the true market price of a security, also known as price discovery. Shorting also provides liquidity to markets and helps hedge your long positions.

When you want to short a stock, your broker lends it to you to sell. When the stock falls, you can sell the stock back to the broker to make a profit.

It is important as a trader to be flexible and that means being able to take short positions as well as long. However, it is also wise to realize that shorting stocks is a very dangerous activity.

The reward for buying a stock is potentially infinite; however for a short, the potential reward is capped at 100% (with an infinite potential for loss). It makes sense, therefore, to put even more research into the stocks that you want to short and to carefully measure how many shorts you hold in your portfolio.

Over time, shorting stocks does not always improve returns on your portfolio but they do help smooth out your equity curve so that you experience smaller drawdowns. It is best to evaluate how many shorts you want in your portfolio and have a number of rules for picking the best ones.

SOME TIPS FROM THE TOP

Over the years, and by doing a fair amount of reading and learning, you soon work out whose voice in the markets you can trust and whose you can't. Everyone has their own favorite traders but I've included here some tips from some of the best traders around.

Jim Rogers: ''Wait till there is money lying in the corner and go over there and pick it up.''

Rogers made a name for himself as co-founder of the Quantum fund with George Soros and has made a lot of money in commodities. He believes in finding trades that are severely 'depressed'.

George Soros: "It takes courage to be a pig."

Soros believes when you have conviction about a trade you should be bold and bet big. He also said, "The way to attain truly superior long-term returns is to grind it out until you're up 30 or 40 percent, and then if you have the conviction, go for a 100 percent year."

Ed Seykota: "Everyone gets what they want out of the market."

Seykota was an early pioneer of computer trading and is a very good systems trader with somewhat of a cult following. He also believes that the main thing holding people back from making money in the markets are themselves.

Jesse Livermore: "Don't fight the tape..

One of the most famous traders of all time and immortalized in the book, Reminiscences of a Stock Operator, Livermore made and lost many millions during his career. He refrained from using the words bullish or bearish and preferred to follow the markets' directions, cutting losses quickly before they got out of control.

William Eckhardt: "...professionals go broke taking small profits."

Eckhardt has been in the business for over 40 years, so it's fair to say he knows a thing or two about trading. "One common adage... that is completely wrongheaded is: You can't go broke taking profits. That's precisely how many traders do go broke. While amateurs go broke by taking large losses, professionals go broke by taking small profits." The essence of this statement is to let your winners run and cut your losses short. If you don't make enough money from your winners you might not last too long.

Meyer Rothschild: "Buy when there is blood on the streets."

German banker Rothschild made his fortune during Napoleonic times. He is quoted as saying you should buy when there is 'blood on the streets, panic, chaos' and he always sold 'too soon'.

Bruce Kovner: "Michael Marcus taught me one other thing that is absolutely critical: You have to be willing to make mistakes regularly; there is nothing wrong with it. Michael taught me about making your best judgment, being wrong, making your next best judgment, being wrong, making your third best judgment, and then doubling your money."

Kovner is another top trader who made a killing in 2008 as markets imploded.

Warren Buffett: "There are two rules of investing. Rule #1–Don't lose money. Rule #2–Never forget Rule #1."

As you can tell Buffett is a firm believer that you should do everything you can to avoid losing money.

Dr. Alexander Elder: "Records are more important to your success than any indicator, system, or technical tools."

Elder elaborates further that "Even the best system is bound to have some holes, but good records will allow you to find them and plug them up."

> Peter Lynch: "If you're in the right sector at the right time, you can make a lot of money very fast."

Expert advice from one of the best stock pickers of all time.

> Van K. Tharp: "There is a strong psychological bias to be right about what we do with our investment. In most people, this bias greatly overrides the desire to make a profit overall in our approach, or it inhibits us from reaching our true profit potential. Most people have overwhelming needs to control the market. As a result, they end up with the market controlling them."

As evident from Tharp's books and advice, the psychological aspects of trading are among the hardest to master. Be confident in your trades and you'll have a fighting chance.

CHAPTER 5:
TECHNICAL ANALYSIS

WHAT IS TECHNICAL ANALYSIS?

Technical analysis is a method for forecasting the direction of prices through the analysis of past market data, primarily using price and volume. It can also be referred to as price trading or trading off the chart.

Fundamental factors underpin markets and are ultimately responsible for where markets head, however, fundamental shifts often take a long time to come to fruition. Traders need a little more help in making decisions. Technical analysis provides the perfect balance for traders looking to sharpen up their timing.

As you can imagine, technical analysis is an immensely broad and subjective topic. (I have done my fair bit of technical trading in the past and so included in this book are some of the strategies that I have found to be worthwhile.)

Price action trading

Essentially, price action trading is based on the concept of behavioral analysis – the idea that since markets are made up of human participants, price alone should be considered the most important indicator of market movement.

As such, price action traders make trading decisions based on price and may ignore other factors such as fundamentals or lagging technical indicators, like moving averages. This concept is often referred to among floor traders as 'reading the tape' and is one of the oldest and most popular methods around for analyzing markets.

A price action trader bases trading decisions on certain patterns that they apply to markets, and use volume to support the analysis. The most important price action patterns are shown here:

Trend lines

Trend lines are possibly the first thing a price action trader looks at when analyzing markets, since they clearly show where markets have been in the past and where they are likely to go in the future.

In theory, a trend line can be drawn to connect any two points. However to be of any worth, trend lines need to connect at least two historical lows or highs. Once in place, trend lines show clear support and resistance levels in a market. Once broken, they signal a change in direction for the security.

Since they are drawn by hand, trend lines can be subjective to the trader. Nevertheless, they do provide the building blocks of trading by price action.

Example: Trend lines should be drawn to connect a low (or a high) and at least one other higher low (or lower high). The trend line here shows strong support, a break of the line would be bearish. Source: IG Index.

Support and resistance levels

Price action traders often rely on important levels of support and resistance in the markets with which to base their trading decisions. Typically, strong levels of support and resistance come from calculations made from a security's price history (for example pivot points or Camarilla levels), strong levels in the markets, such as yesterday's high or the previous month's low, or even significant double '00' levels (such as 1500 or 1.30).

Never underestimate the importance of some of these double '00' levels as markets often hit them – if nothing else, than to get rid of all the stops that are placed there.

Once a trader knows the key levels of support and resistance, he or she can use the levels as entry points, take profit levels or stop loss levels – depending on where they see markets heading.

Breakouts

A breakout occurs when the price of a security moves beyond predetermined support or resistance levels and usually indicates a strong bullish or bearish move in the respective direction. Often, a breakout occurs after a period of consolidation in the market or when a security trades within a relatively clear trading range or channel. Price action traders are also aware of breakout pull backs, where the market often retraces a certain amount after a break-out occurs; breakout failures occur when the breakout is not supported by large volume.

Reversals

Reversal patterns are a common feature of markets and typically occur when a market has moved in a direction for such an amount of time that the move has become exhausted and threatens to move back in the opposite direction sharply. They differ from mere retracements by the fact that they last longer and offer more poten-tial to profit. They also come in many forms.

Head-and-shoulders, double tops, double bottoms, and rising and falling wedges are all examples of possible reversal patterns.

Example: A double top formation. A trader should only enter a short if the market moves below the neck line. Source: finviz.com.

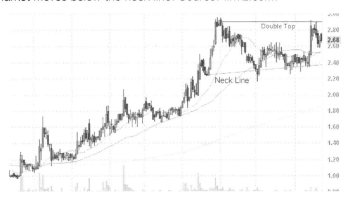

Example: The chart below shows an example of a double bottom formation. The stock found support at the double bottom before taking off.
Source: finviz.com.

Bilateral triangles

Bilateral patterns are often identified by triangle patterns that fit over
the chart and indicate that a period of consolidation for a market is
likely coming to an end. The triangles can be ascending, descend-
ing or symmetrical. However, their common feature is that they are
usually coming together to form a converging apex point. At some
point a market needs to break, either to the up-side or down-side,
and when it does, it's a strong signal that a market has found its
next long-term direction.

Example: The chart below shows two converging trend lines moving
towards an apex point. The break of this upper line shows a strong signal
to go long. Source: IG Index.

Gaps

Many price action traders perceive gaps in markets as important indicators of market strengths or weaknesses. Indeed, gaps are usually the result of lots of traders moving to just one side of the trade and, therefore, indicate a major turn in market sentiment, especially when accompanied by high volume. They nearly always offer strong clues to the next direction a market is going, so gaps should be taken seriously when they occur.

Volume

Most price action traders make volume a key consideration when analyzing a market on price alone, since it is volume that determines whether a move is simply a technical reaction or is actually supported by a large number of market participants. It's for this reason traders talk about a market 'spiking up' on 'heavy' volume.

Volume describes the number of financial transactions that change hands on a given day. So if a lot of people come together to trade at one time and the result is a clear bullish or bearish move, it's a signal to trade in the same direction.

HOW TO DAY TRADE USING PIVOT POINTS

Professional day traders have been using pivot points to trade the markets since the days of the trading floor. Back then, complicated technical indicators were not as freely available, so traders relied on watching the tape and a couple of calculated levels called pivots. Since pivot point levels are so widely watched, they often manage to predict turning points in the market with extraordinary accuracy.

Pivot points can be used by traders in different ways and are generally combined with support and resistance levels: R1, R2 and R3; S1, S2 and S3. Each point is based on the previous day's trading levels and can be calculated using a simple equation.

<u>Calculation</u>

Pivot (P) = (High + Low + Close) / 3

The pivot point uses the previous day's high, low and close and is the mark from which all support and resistance levels are based. If a market trades under the pivot, it is generally a bearish indicator, while if it trades above the pivot, the market is in bullish mode. The pivot itself often acts as a strong level of support or resistance.

R1 = P + (P − Low)

The first level of resistance (R1) is calculated using the pivot and yesterday's low. It forms the first level where a market might be nearing an overbought condition.

S1 = P − (High − P)

Likewise, the first level of support (S1) represents the first level whereby traders might want to become bullish on a market.

R2 = P + (High − Low)

The second resistance level (R2) is higher than the first and determined from the full width of the previous day's trading range.

S2 = P − (High − Low)

The second support level (S2) is exactly like R2 but in reverse and offers an even stronger level of support than S1.

R3 = High + 2×(P − Low)

The third resistance level (R3) is calculated by doubling the range of the previous day and gives a level that offers even stronger resistance.

S3 = Low − 2×(High − P)

The third support level (S3) is calculated in the same way as R3. The further away the support and resistance levels get the less likely markets hit those points.

Using pivot points

Pivot points are always important market levels but are generally used by traders in different ways.

Typically, resistance levels are used as points to sell into a market and support levels places to buy.

However, the levels are also used by traders to indicate good points to place stops or to take profits. Similarly, pivot levels can be used as entry points for trend traders, just as well as for range traders. If the price smashes through a pivot point with a lot of strength, a trend trader may just as happily buy the market on the first resistance, as a range trader might sell.

As well as this, pivot points can be combined with other indicators such as moving averages or calculated using more complex formulas to give supposedly better entry points.

Following are three examples of pivot points in action (taken over the same period):

EUR/USD

As can be seen in the next chart, pivot points often produce uncanny levels in which to enter a market. In the hourly chart below, the pivot for EUR/USD (1.2805) on March 29, would have been an excellent place to buy and would have made nearly 20 pips on what was a quiet day of trading.

On the previous day, the market bounced nicely off the first resistance level and would have given a trader who was short at this level a quick and easy 20 pips.

The day prior also shows the uncanny ability of pivot points to find the key levels in the market. EUR/USD smashed through the pivot in the morning, through the first support and second support and then consolidated around the third support. A trader who sold EUR/USD as it smashed through the pivot could have used S1 and S2 to bring down his stop levels and used S3 as a great take profit level.

Example #1: EUR/USD. 1-hour chart with pivots. Source: IG Index

USD/JPY

During the same period, the pivot also acted as a strong level for USD/JPY. On March 29 the market fluctuated around the mark for most of the day. The market did not quite hit the first support level in what was a quiet day's trading due to a public holiday.

However, on the previous day, the market bounced strongly off the first support level (93.92). In fact, the pivot (94.42) and first support offered an excellent guide to the day's range.

A similar story unfolded on the day prior. USD/JPY moved up towards R1 in the morning before trading through the pivot and then bouncing back off the first support level. The market then began to return back to the pivot point.

Example #2: USD/JPY. 1 hour chart with pivots. Source: IG Index.

EUR/GBP

As can be seen by the hourly chart below, there were also great opportunities in EUR/GBP for trading pivot levels.

On March 27, the market dropped through the pivot early on and then proceeded to the first support level and later onto the second support level. A trader could easily have sold EUR/GBP on the pivot, (placing his stop a few ticks above the pivot), then used S1 and S2 as levels to take profit. Either option would have given the trader a good day's profit.

The next day was also good for pivot traders with the market bouncing off the first support level (84.26) aggressively, and hitting the pivot in a short amount of time. The market then took off again until it hit the first resistance level. It then reversed and proceeded to return back towards S1. As can be seen, pivot points can work especially well in volatile conditions.

Example #3: EUR/GBP. 1-hour chart with pivots. Source: IG Index.

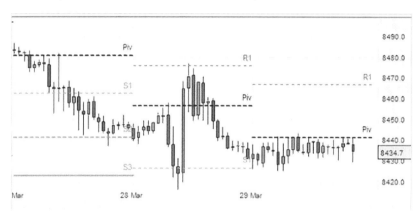

Since pivot points use data from the previous day's trading, they are continuously adapting to the characteristics and volatility of markets. This means that the key pivots and support and resistance levels are never too far away from the action. Traders, therefore, nearly always have an opportunity to make a profit.

Whether used as entry points, price targets or stop loss levels, the sheer importance of pivot points lies in their ability to adapt to market conditions and the fact that they are watched by so many professional traders.

HOW TO TRADE WITH JAPANESE CANDLESTICKS

Japanese candlestick charts are thought to have been invented in the 18th century by a Japanese rice trader known as Munehisa Homma. Each bar of a candlestick chart is able to display the open, high, low and close prices for a given time interval and are thus able to show the trading range for a period of time.

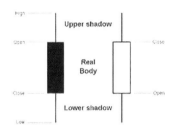

Today, they are the most popular way of viewing financial data since they are able to convey much more information than other graphs such as line or bar charts.

A candlestick is composed of a body and an upper and lower shadow, known as the wick. The wick demonstrates the highest and lowest prices a market traded at during the particular time interval, while the body shows the opening and closing prices of a market.

If a market is above the open, the candlestick has a white or green body, whereas, if a market is below the open, the body is black or red. Similarly, if the market closes exactly where it opened, the candle has no body at all.

In order to trade using Japanese candlesticks, it is essential to know the different candlestick patterns and what they mean.

Spinning top

The spinning top pattern is characterized by a small body and long wicks on both sides. It shows that a market has gone up, gone down and then ended up pretty much where it started. It shows the market is undecided and is not sure where to go next.

Doji

Similar to spinning tops, dojis often indicate reversals since they represent markets with a lot of uncertainty.

A doji with a long wick, where the open price matches the close, shows a lot of indecision and is called a long-legged doji.

This is a gravestone doji. The market has been up but has rejected the higher levels and signals a major turning point in the trend may be near.

Dragonfly is opposite to the gravestone doji. The market has gone lower but closes near its highs, meaning the downtrend may likely be nearly over.

White marubozu

A white marubozu occurs when a market opens, then climbs strongly and finishes the day near its highs. It's represented by a large white or green body with no wick and it's a strongly bullish indication.

Black marubozu

Likewise, a black marubozu occurs when the market finishes near its lows and is a bearish indicator, since it shows a market is moving in a strongly downward fashion.

Hammer

A candle can only be called a hammer when it occurs during a downtrend. In this situation the market trades down to its lows but then finishes back where it started. As such, the market is said to be 'hammering out a bottom' and is a very good reversal indicator. It's usually wise to wait another couple of bars for confirmation before trading on the basis of one candle alone.

Hanging man

A hanging man indicates a possible top in a market and can be a sign of a possible reversal in an uptrend. Although the market has finished near its highs, the long tail down, indicates that sellers are coming in and beginning to outnumber the buyers. Once again, the candle should only be acted upon with confirmation from another signal or indicator.

Shooting star and inverted hammer

A shooting star occurs when the price moves higher in the midst of an upward trend but ends the day near its lows. In other words,

the market has moved up but has been unable to sustain the move leading to sellers driving it back down. It's a strong reversal indicator.

An inverted hammer occurs during a downward market. The market is bought up but sellers are able to bring the market back down. However, there are not enough sellers to keep the market going lower, therefore its likely buyers can regain control of the market soon.

Bullish and bearish engulfing

A bullish engulfing pattern occurs when a bearish candle is immediately followed by a strong Maribozu or bullish candle. It signals that a strong uptrend may be on the cards, since buyers have managed to outnumber sellers strongly.

Similarly, a bearish engulfing pattern occurs when a bullish candle is immediately followed by a strong bearish candle and indicates the trend may change downwards.

Three white soldiers and three black crows

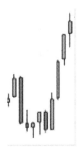

There are triple patterns too. Three white solders occurs during a downtrend when markets are declining but are then hit with three solid bullish candles, signaling the beginning of a strong upwards move. To be considered valid, the first candle must be a reversal, with the second candle being larger than the first. Additionally, the third candle should be at least as big as the second and all candles should finish near their highs with little shadow showing.

Three black crows are essentially the opposite of three white soldiers. For the pattern to be considered valid, the crows must occur during an upward trend with the first candle being a reversal. The second candle should finish near its lows and be bigger than the first and the third candle should be at least as big as the second candle. All the candles should finish near their lows with little to no shadow. The less shadow (or wick) there is, the stronger the move is likely to be.

<u>Morning star</u>

A morning star needs the following character-istics to be valid. Firstly, a market must be in a downtrend and have a bearish candle. This should then be followed by a doji of some kind, indicating indecision in the market. The third candle should then be a strong, bullish candle. This is a clear indication that the downtrend is coming to an end and the market is reversing.

As well as these patterns, there are others such as evening stars, tweezer patterns, three inside up, three inside down. Candlesticks should never be used to trade on their own but they are excellent tools to have in the armory.

HOW TO TRADE WITH BOLLINGER BANDS

Bollinger Bands were invented by the analyst John Bollinger in the 1980s and are another popular tool used by traders to analyze the markets.

Bollinger Bands are placed two standard deviations away from the simple moving average and are excellent measures of volatility. The bands seek to provide a relative definition of what is high and what is low and are adaptive to markets. In this way, they can be incorpo-rated into several different types of trading strategies.

Default parameters consist of 20 periods and two standard deviations but can be adjusted as necessary. The inventor, John Bollinger, also provides 22 rules for using the bands. The most important rules are provided here, the rest can be found online at www.bollingerbands.com

Bollinger Bands can be used to compare price action and indicator action, to arrive at rigorous buy and sell decisions.

In other words, Bollinger Bands can be devised along with other technical indicators to provide buy and sell signals. However, the success of any strategy relies on the combination of various indicators and using the correct settings for each market. Some traders may find success buying or selling a market when it breaks out of the bands, whereas some traders may use the bands as reversal opportunities.

Tags of the bands are just that, tags not signals. A tag of the upper Bollinger Band is NOT in-and-of-itself a sell signal. A tag of the lower Bollinger Band is NOT in-and-of-itself a buy signal.

When the market touches one of the bands, it signals the price is either high or low. It does not necessarily indicate a buy or sell signal although strategies can be devised to use the bands in such a way. They can also be combined with other indicators to further develop break out or mean reversion systems.

In trending markets, price can (and does) walk up the upper Bollinger Band and down the lower Bollinger Band.

Buying into the market when it hits the lower Bollinger Band or selling when it touches the upper band is best for choppy markets, with no real direction. However, for trending markets like USD/JPY above, the price often moves along the upper or lower band with great consistency.

Closes outside the Bollinger Bands are initially continuation signals, not reversal signals. This has been the basis for many successful volatility breakout systems.

When a market closes outside the Bollinger Band, it is first a signal of a breakout and not a reversal. This means that a trade should be entered in the direction of the breakout and not in the opposite direction. A reversal trade should be entered only if the market then comes back inside the band and starts to move back to the middle.

BandWidth has many uses. Its most popular use is to identify 'the squeeze' but is also useful in identifying trend changes.

In the Bollinger Band, BandWidth is used to indicate how wide the Bollinger Bands are and is normalized using the middle band. The BandWidth is four times the coefficient of variation using the default parameters.

When volatility drops, the Bollinger Bands come closer together and form a squeeze scenario. When this happens, an explosive directional move is never far away.

Mean reversion

The most obvious way to use Bollinger Bands in a trading system is to sell when the market touches the upper band and buy when the price touches the lower band. Since these levels show that the market is high or low compared to the mean, it is likely to move back sooner or later. Traders can either look to the middle moving average line to take profits or wait till the market moves to the opposite band.

Breakouts

Another way to use Bollinger Bands is as part of a trend following strategy. In this scenario, if the price closes outside of one of the bands, it can be said that a breakout has occurred. This shows significant strength and indicates that the market is likely to carry on this direction for a while. Thus, if the market closes above the upper band, a trader should enter a long position on the next open. Conversely, if the market closes below the lower band, a trader should enter a short position. The moving average middle line can then be used as an area to place a stop.

Volatility

It is also possible to use Bollinger Bands in a volatility system by watching for times when the Bollinger Bands are either very close together or very spaced apart. Often, when markets are quiet, Bollinger Bands come together in a pincer motion. When this happens, it is almost always a sure-fire signal that markets are about to explode either up or down.

Similarly, if the market has recently experienced a lot of volatility and the bands are very far apart, you can bet your life that the market will settle down and move into a more reliable range in the near future.

Bollinger Bands can be used in many ways and they are not necessarily restricted to price charts. They can also provide interesting signals when used against volume, momentum, or other sentiment indicators. As such, they are one of the most flexible indicators around. As with most technical indicators it pays to become creative and think of new ways to use them.

HOW TO TRADE PULLBACK PATTERNS

Quite simply, a pullback pattern occurs any time a price is seen to fall back from its recent peak. They are best identified when there is a prevailing upward trend, since they indicate the market is correcting slightly, giving a trader a chance to join the trend, before it continues on its way up.

In this way, pullback patterns are used in many strategies that attempt to join the trend at lower prices than have previously been available. The term 'pullback' is often used interchangeably with 'reversal', 'retracement' and 'correction'.

Although a pullback pattern often signals the perfect opportunity to join an uptrend, it can sometimes lead to danger that every trader needs to be aware of.

Since the pullback is signifying a change in direction, albeit a temporary one, a pullback can sometimes lead to a complete change of trend. When this occurs, buying the pullback fails, since markets continue to drop and the trade makes a loss. A good method is therefore to confirm the pullback with other indicators.

Regression channels

When traders look for pullback patterns, they also look for other patterns and indicators to support their position. Channels are handy for traders since they show the levels at which a pullback may get to and then reverse from.

Regression channels are linear and can be drawn onto a chart manually or placed there using a charting package. They are often used by institutional traders and are effective, since market prices typically drift between the top and lower levels of the channel.

Once a pullback gets underway, a trader waits until the price nears the bottom channel before buying. The trader then keeps his or her position until it nears the top of the channel. This method has another advantage; if the pullback drops significantly below the bottom regression channel, it is a fair assumption that the main trend has changed. A trader can then exit his position and look for another trade in the opposite direction.

One of the main advantages for trading regression channels lies in the fact they are heavily used by institutional traders. Indeed, a number of black box systems trade regression channels.

Example of an upward regression channel. Source: finviz.com

Moving averages within pullbacks

Moving averages are an extremely popular method used by traders to find trends in markets. It is said that when a moving average crosses over a slower average, it signals a strong upward trend.

However, moving averages suffer from a number of issues – they are lagging indicators so they often signal entries too late and they are also prone to whipsaws. Because of this, some traders look for a moving average crossover and then enter a position on the first pullback. This way the trader guarantees trading in the direction of the trend but does not have to face the problem of being whipsawed as a result of buying too high.

Generally, a major trend has a number of smaller pullbacks or corrections along its way up, thus it makes sense to use these fluctuations to join a market. It is exactly the same situation when trading breakout patterns.

However, it must be remembered that the first pullback is always the strongest. Each proceeding pullback weakens in strength and becomes more and more likely to be a change in trend.

HOW TO USE THE MACD INDICATOR

The moving average convergence divergence (or MACD) was invented by famous technical trader Gerard Apel, in 1979. MACD has a number of uses and is very popular among technicians. It can be used as a trend indicator or a momentum indicator, it can measure divergence and it can also be combined successfully with other indicators.

The MACD works by calculating the difference between two moving averages, usually the 26-day and 12-day exponential moving averages (EMA), and is presented on a chart using two lines and a histogram.

MACD

The MACD appears with three numbers next to it, usually 12, 26 and 9.

12 represents the number of bars that is used to calculate the fast moving average and 26 is the number of bars to calculate the slower average. The differences of the two moving averages (12 and 26) are represented by the two lines. The third number (9)

is represented by bars, known as a histogram. This third number represents the difference between the two lines.

A common misconception is that the lines on the MACD represent the moving averages of the price but this is in fact not the case. Rather, the lines represent the moving averages of the difference between the two moving averages.

It can sound quite confusing so let's see how the MACD can be used in trading decisions.

Crossover

A popular way to use the MACD indicator is to use the crossover strategy. This strategy is similar to a normal moving average crossover except with an important difference; the two lines on the MACD are moving averages of the difference between two moving averages. They therefore show if the trend is diverging or converging. Thus, when the fast line crosses above the slower line, the difference between the two averages can be said to be diverging at a faster rate. This signifies momentum and is therefore a strong buy signal.

Conversely, if the fast line crosses under the slower line, it can be said that the difference between the two averages is decreasing or converging. In this situation, market momentum is slowing and is therefore a sell signal. The market is likely to reverse direction at this point.

As can be seen from the next chart, this strategy would have made a nice profit on April 11 of about 40 pips.

When the crossover takes place, the histogram shows a figure of zero since at that point there is no difference between the two lines. Using this variable is the easiest way to incorporate the indicator when programming the strategy into code.

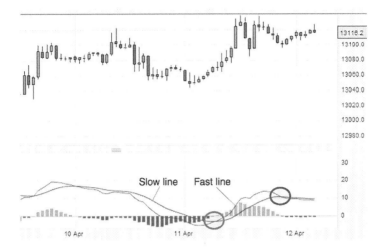

Source: IG Index

Momentum divergence

Another way to use the MACD indicator is to compare momentum within the indicator itself.

Although this method is sometimes forgotten, this is probably how the MACD was meant to be used when it was first invented.

The best way to see the momentum divergence strategy in action is using a stock or market that is making new highs or lows.

Let's say that stock Y is on the up and has just made a new record high. Everything is up – the price, the moving average, the bands. However, a look at the MACD indicator suggests that while the fast moving average has increased, it has done so at a slower rate than the slower moving average. In this instance, it's clear that even though the market is making new highs, it is doing so at a much slower rate. In effect, the two moving averages are converging.

Whenever a stock makes a new high or new low but the MACD indicator does not, the market is shown to be losing momentum and is therefore likely to be near a reversal point. This strategy can work just as well for a downtrend.

A good example of this is shown in the below chart. As you can see, EUR/USD was in a strong downward trend and posting new lows relatively consistently. However, even though the market was making fresh lows, the MACD indicator was actually shown to turn upwards during March and indicated that a change in direction was

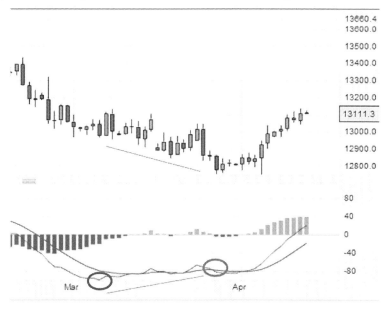

Source: IG Index

imminent. The upward movement of the MACD indicator showed downward momentum was slowing and would have been a good opportunity to buy.

Using the crossover method, the MACD is always a lagging indicator. But the great thing about the momentum divergence strategy is that in this instance, the MACD actually acts as a type of forward indicator. By measuring the rate of change between the averages, it is able to look for the tops and bottoms before they occur.

Limitations of the MACD indicator

There are a number of advantages and disadvantages that you should know before you start using the MACD.

Disadvantages

The main disadvantage of the MACD indicator is subjectivity.

Like many technical indicators, the MACD has settings that can be changed to give almost limitless numbers of variations, which means results always differ from person to person. A trader must decide for example what moving averages to choose.

The suggested settings are the 12-day moving average, 26-day and 9-day, however, these can easily be changed. A trader must know what time frame the MACD works best on and there are no easy answers, since the MACD tends to work differently across different markets. Generally, however, the MACD works best when it is confirmed across several different time frames – especially further out time frames such as the weekly chart.

Lagging indicator

Unless using the momentum divergence strategy which seeks to pick tops and bottoms before they occur, the MACD has an inherent disadvantage that occurs with all technical indicators that concern price history.

Since moving averages are lagging indicators, in that they measure the change in a stock price over a period of time (in the past), they tend to be late at giving signals. Often, when a fast moving average crosses over a slower one, the market has already turned upwards some days ago.

When the MACD crossover finally gives a buy signal, it has already missed some of the gain. In the worst case scenario it gets whipsawed when the market turns back the other way. The best way to get around this problem is to use longer-term charts such as hourly or daily charts (since these tend to have fewer whipsaws). It is also a good idea to use other indicators or time frames to confirm the signals.

Early signals

While the crossover strategy has the limitation of being a lagging indicator, the momentum divergence strategy has the opposite problem. Namely, it can signal a reversal too early causing too many small losing trades before hitting the big one.

The problem arises since a converging or diverging trend does not always lead to a reversal. Indeed, often a market converges for just a bar or two catching its breath before it picks up momentum again and continues its trend.

The solution to such limitations, once more, is to combine it with other indicators and use different confirmation techniques. The ultimate test is to set the MACD up in code and test the indicator yourself on historical data. That way you are able to find out when and in which situations and conditions the indicator works best.

HOW TO USE THE RSI INDICATOR

Relative strength indicator (RSI) is a versatile momentum indicator and is one of the most popular technical analysis indicators.

The indicator uses a formula to calculate the magnitude of recent losses to recent gains, in an effort to tell when a market is likely to be at an overbought or oversold level.

The formula itself is simple and calculated as below, then presented as an oscillator:

RSI = 100 – 100(1 + RS)

In this instance RS refers to the average of a stock or asset's day up closes, divided by the average of the stock or asset's day down closes. As so:

RS = Average of days' up closes / average of days' down closes.

Using this formula, it is possible to garner values stretching from

0-100. These values are then used to represent momentum within a market which can be plotted directly below the price chart in the form of an oscillator.

In theory, the higher or lower the value of the oscillator, the stronger the momentum within a market. In practice, due to the way the formula is calculated, the RSI rarely goes higher than 80, or lower than 20. It is therefore much more common to use the levels 70 and 30 for trading decisions.

Thus, when the RSI is above 70, a market is deemed to be in an overbought condition and when it is below 30, a market is oversold. The best strategy is, therefore, to initiate a buy when RSI crosses under 30 and to go short when RSI crosses over 70.

This is the typical way to use the RSI, however the indicator can also be used in the reverse way, in order to follow trends. Using this method, a trader buys a market when the RSI crosses over 70 and does not sell until it crosses back under 30. Conversely, you can short a market when the RSI crosses under 30 and buy back when it crosses over 70.

Divergence

As well as measuring momentum, the RSI can indicate divergence. For example, let's say a currency has made a new high but the RSI has just turned down (it has not made a new high). In this case, a market is showing signs of decreasing momentum – even though the price has gone up, it has not been accompanied with an increasing RSI.

This is a clear signal of divergence and signals a reversal in a market is likely.

HOW TO USE THE DMI INDICATOR

The directional movement index or directional movement indicator (DMI) is another powerful tool for analyzing price movement and identifying trends. It was developed by J. Welles Wilder in 1978.

Make-up of the DMI

While looking at the lines of the DMI may be daunting initially, the principles behind it are simple and can be understood with relative ease.

The DMI works on the basis of a moving average which is recorded using two lines. The first line is the positive directional movement indicator or +DMI, and the other is the negative directional movement indicator or –DMI.

As their names would suggest, the former is a measurement of the strength of a bullish or upward movement in price, while the latter measures bearish or downward movement.

To elaborate further: The +DMI rises and falls as price rises and falls; the –DMI does the opposite by rising when price falls and falling when price rises.

The line which appears higher than the other is sometimes referred to as the dominant DMI and is simply the stronger of the two; the DMI which is more likely to determine which direction price will move in.

Interpreting the DMI

When the +DMI and –DMI cross over, this signals a change in trend and many traders use this, in conjunction with other indicators, to determine when to enter or exit a market.

Some less experienced traders may use the DMI crossover as their sole entry or exit signal, but it is important to understand that while the DMI is an excellent tool it can sometimes provide false signals.

It is, therefore, a good idea to use it in combination with various other tools.

Qualifying DMI signals

Although high volatility lends itself to more pronounced DMI movement, this can often result in late signals being presented.

There are instances where you observe several consecutive DMI crossovers; however, one way of determining the legitimacy of a signal like this is to look at the mean price.

The mean price is depicted with a central line on the DMI and can be used to assess the strength of price movement.

DMI strength is measured on a scale of 0-100 and when either the +DMI or –DMI surpass a value of 25. This is typically considered a strong indication and a fairly reliable signal of a shift in the trend.

When looking at the line which has passed above the mean price line, you should also keep a close eye on the other line. So if the +DMI passes beyond a value of 25, watch to see how the –DMI behaves. A growing expansion between the two lines strongly suggests that it is time to either open or close your position.

Rules for trading the DMI

Crossover rule

When the DMI+ and DMI- lines cross over, this often signals that a trend reversal is due to occur, and can be a sign for you to either open or close your position; however, it should be qualified further before doing anything hasty.

Extreme point rule

When you notice a crossover taking place, you should use the extreme price point as the reversal price. If we were long, our reversal point would be the lowest price observed during the trading period in which the crossover took place.

Using the extreme point rule enables you to set parameters on your trade, so that you can open your position or set your stop loss at a level which is appropriate to the current price action, thus minimizing your losses if the crossover signal should prove to be false.

Applying the ADX indicator

We can further qualify the signal by applying the average directional index (ADX), also developed by Wilder, as this enables us to gather even more evidence to strengthen the case for a trend reversal. When ADX moves above both –DMI and +DMI, it is a sign that a reversal is likely.

POSITIVE VOLUME INDEX

The positive volume index (PVI) dates back to the 1930s. Paul L. Dysart generated the PVI through the advance-decline line in order to come up with a reliable indicator that could be incorporated into any trading strategy. He then presented it in an advisory publication, called Tradeways, until his death in 1969. Although the PVI was popular among market technicians, Norman G. Fosback developed the theory further in Stock Market Logic and significantly increased the popularity of the theory by applying it to individual securities.

What is the PVI and NVI?

The PVI and NVI (negative volume index) are called price accumulation volume indicators. The PVI is based on the assumption that active stock market days are driven by uninformed crowds and less active stock market days are supposedly driven by smart money decisions. Smarter investors, more specifically referred to money from institutions and professional traders, are more likely to make moves during quieter days.

How is the PVI calculated?

To calculate the PVI, you have to calculate price movements during increased volume. When the volume is greater today than it was yesterday, then:

PVI = {[(today's closing price-yesterday's closing price) / yesterday's closing price)] x previous PVI}

When the volume is the same or less than yesterday, then PVI remains unchanged. Typically, the PVI is compared to a 255-day moving average of its value (which roughly works out as a year, when taking out public holidays and weekends).

What is the purpose of the PVI?

The purpose of the PVI is to identify bull and bear markets and thereby help traders choose (at the very least) which side of the market to trade on.

When the PVI is above its 1-year moving average, or when it crosses over the average, it is a very good sign that a bull market is taking place. A trader should therefore be looking to buy the market when it does so.

When the PVI is below its 1-year moving average, the probability of a bear market is at 67% indicating that a trader should sell his positions (if long) and consider shorting the market.

This is a clear signal of a bear market which stood up to a number of scientific tests by Dysart during the 1950s and 1960s.

Dysart also proved that the indicator works better when combined with the NVI. So while the PVI analyzes uninformed investors, the NVI analyzes smarter investors. He also came up with another rule to further hone the strategy by stating that "signals are most authentic when the NVI has moved sideways for a number of months in a relatively narrow range."

Added benefits

The beauty of the PVI is that unlike other technical indicators, it provides signals that are based on something other than price. This makes it valuable since it gives another dimension to predicting the market and works well when combined with indicators that are price sensitive.

It's also a robust indicator, with settings that should not be changed to suit markets. The settings have been derived to work on daily volumes, meaning any other time frame and the PVI should not be deemed accurate. This greatly improves reliability, especially when compared with some other indicators that have thousands of different setting combinations.

How to trade using the PVI

A simple strategy would therefore consist of waiting for the PVI to cross over its 255-day EMA before entering a long position. The crossover indicates that uninformed investors are joining in with the smart ones and pushing the market higher.

Conversely, when the PVI crosses under its EMA, a trader can initiate a short position and hope to profit from the coming bear market.

Similarly, if the PVI is above its EMA line then there is a 79% chance of the market being in a bull phase.

As such, the PVI is an effective tool for discerning the type of market phase.

Once the PVI is used to determine whether the market is bullish or bearish, a trader can use this information to his/her advantage and only enter trades in the direction of that trend.

The Negative Volume Index

As PVI's sister indicator, it is of course handy to know about the NVI, which is essentially the same as the PVI but for times when volume in markets are decreasing. It is at those times that smart investors are supposed to be acting in the markets and signalling the building up of new positions. However, the NVI should also be known for how it works in conjunction with the PVI, since supportive signals from both indicators lead to much better signals overall. In other words, if the PVI and NVI both experience crossovers at the same time, then the quality of the signal is much stronger and a trader can be much more confident about making the trade.

TREND FOLLOWING WITH MOVING AVERAGES

We have already talked about trend following, here I explain a simple technique that traders use to take advantage of this well-known strategy.

The concept behind trend following is that financial markets tend to exhibit trends that can be exploited for profit. Due to global imbalances, supply/demand constraints and long tail events, such trends often tend to last longer than one would normally expect, allowing significant opportunities for trend followers.

The successful trend follower is therefore able to make money, not by studying the fundamentals, but by spotting trends using technical indicators and then jumping on the trend and riding the wave to its conclusion.

Generally, trend followers miss the bottom or the top of a market but they often catch a big chunk of the middle.

Moving averages

Moving averages are used to show the average value of a security's price over a set period of time. They are easy to calculate as you just add up the closing prices of a security over a certain number of periods then divide by the number of periods. Nearly all charting applications do this for you and they usually offer different types of moving averages too, such as exponential and weighted averages.

Moving averages, though, are an extremely popular tool among trend followers and traders since they act to solve a number of problems that are inherent when trying to predict financial markets.

First, moving averages are able to show the direction of a market much more objectively than the drawing of trend lines or using the naked eye. Since they use the true price sequence of a market, they offer a clear picture of the real direction of the market without being influenced by small movements.

Second, moving averages are useful since they filter out noise and smooth data. This means traders can see the real trend of markets and not be thrown off course every time the market spikes up or down against the trend.

Now we know the advantages of using moving averages, we can see how they are used by traders to find trends.

Moving average crossovers

The most common method used by trend followers to spot a trend is by watching for the crossover of two different timed moving averages. This method can easily be seen on any price chart.

When a faster moving average (such as a 20-day MA), crosses over a slower moving average (such as a 50-day MA) it signals that a market is trending higher, since the most recent price data shows the market moving higher, more quickly than the older price data. This is clearly shown in the daily chart below. Source: IG Index.

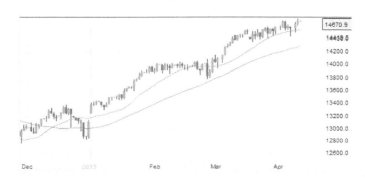

As you can see, the 20-day MA crossed over the 50-day MA on December 13, signaling a new uptrend was in place. The trend follower would have bought on this signal and stayed long until the faster moving average crossed back under the slower moving average.

When the faster moving average crosses under the slower moving average, it is a signal that a downtrend has started. In this case a trend follower will either close his long position or enter a new short position on the crossover.

One of the most popular references to the moving average crossover is when the 50-day EMA crosses over the 200-day EMA, known as the 'golden cross' – a strongly bullish signal. Likewise, the 'death cross' occurs when the 50 day EMA crosses under the 200 and is seen as very bearish.

Just one moving average

Crossovers are probably the most common method used by traders, however, there are other uses for moving averages in trend following. Some traders, for example, enter a long position when the price jumps above just one moving average. They then exit when the price drops back below the MA. Using the chart above as an example, a trader would therefore buy the market as it jumped above the 20-day MA on January 1, 2013. He would then close the position when the market dropped back below the MA on February 19, making a substantial profit.

As well as this, moving averages can also be used as a guide for placing stops or as confirmation signals or filters for other trend following strategies. They can also be used in mean reversion strategies by trading in the opposite way when a crossover takes place. There are plenty of possibilities to try out.

DIFFERENT TYPES OF MOVING AVERAGES

However good moving averages are for identifying trading opportunities, they do have one inherent flaw – which is that they are lagging indicators.

In other words, by using past data, they only identify a trend once it has already occurred. The problem is, speeding up a moving average leads to overshooting the market and more whipsaws. Designing a moving average then, is a trade off between lag and curve smoothness. There are several types of moving averages out there that aim to solve this issue.

Simple moving average

The simple moving average (SMA) is the moving average everyone knows. It takes the simple average of the last X number of periods, which means it is stable and signals trend changes relatively slowly.

Exponential moving average

The exponential moving average (EMA) is probably the most popular moving average. It works just like the SMA but its formula gives more weight to recent values. What this means is that it responds more quickly to recent price moves than those further away. As such, lag is reduced and the EMA line is able to respond to the market trend more quickly.

Triple exponential moving average

As the name suggests, this average seeks to reduce the lag of a typical EMA by tripling the weighting of recent prices. The triple exponential average (TEMA) is thus able to respond to market moves even quicker than the EMA or SMA. However, because of this, it sometimes overshoots the market and is therefore not as smooth a filter. Overshooting leads to more whipsaws and unstable trade signals.

Adaptive moving average

The adaptive moving average (AMA) came about as a result of trying to improve on the original exponential moving average. Perry Kaufman expanded on the EMA by multiplying the weighting of the EMA by a volatility factor. By doing so, the AMA seeks to adapt more quickly to the market by indicating when volatility conditions change.

Hull moving average

Trader Alan Hull's attempt to solve the problem of lag versus smoothness, comes in the form of the Hull moving average (Hull MA). Hull uses several weighted averages in his formula and claims by doing so he is able to reduce lag and increase smoothness at the same time.

Jurik moving average

The Jurik moving average (JMA), from Jurik research, is a less well-known moving average that is thought to be used by some institutional traders. The makers of the JMA claim the formula is based on military research that uses computers to track moving enemy targets. Jurik say the MA is smooth and virtually lag free, the best moving average on the market. However, the formula is a kept secret which can only be purchased as a locked indicator.

From my own experience, the Hull MA works well and is superior to the SMA. JMA is fast although a more complex indicator and the EMA seems to perform as well as any. I told you technical analysis was a broad subject.

WILLIAMS PERCENT RANGE (WPR) OSCILLATOR

Unlike the moving average, which is most commonly used to spot the beginning and end of a trend, the Williams percent range (WPR) indicator is an overbought/oversold oscillator more associated with the strategy of mean reversion.

Essentially, the WPR oscillator works rather like the relative strength index (RSI). Developed by Larry Williams, WPR, uses a scale of values that fluctuate between 0 (strongly overbought) and -100 (strongly oversold) to indicate the overall condition of the market. The oscillator is calculated using a combination of the current closing price, the lowest low of a certain number of periods and the highest high of the same number of periods. It can be worked out as follows:

First, choose a period "N" for "%R" (e.g. 14)

Then, use the formula:

$$\%R = 100 * (HN - CCP) / (HN - LN)$$

Where:

CCP = current closing price

LN = lowest low of past "N" periods

HN = highest high of past "N" periods.

Interpretation

Understanding the WPR oscillator is pretty easy. Basically, whenever the oscillator is between the values 0 and -20, the market is overbought. In such a condition, a trader should be very cautious about buying the market, and should consider closing his position if long.

Likewise, whenever the oscillator is between -80 and -100, the market is oversold and represents a good opportunity to buy.

As can be seen from the chart below, the WPR oscillator often has an uncanny ability for showing the turning points in the market.

Source: IG Index.

Of course, no technical indicator is foolproof and using the WPR oscillator occasionally leads to false trends or reversals.

However, by testing different settings and combining indicators together, it may be possible to find ways to harness the power of these trading tools and reap the rewards.

HOW TO TRADE PARABOLIC MOVES

Parabolic moves occur when a market moves up or down in an exponential type way, leading to what looks on a chart like the formation of a parabolic curve. These are very rare moves that typically occur from periods of rampant speculation or at the end of bubbles. They can be hard to trade too, since buying or selling into a parabolic move takes a lot of courage.

However, if done correctly, the benefits of trading a parabolic move can be great as they offer rapid profit potential. Prices tend to move very sharply at the end of a parabolic move.

Identifying a parabolic curve

The key to trading parabolic moves is first being able to identify them correctly. Although the parabolic SAR indicator is sometimes used by traders it is not always effective in finding parabolic moves, so a better option is to simply scan charts with the naked eye.

The first thing you are looking for is a market that is increasing at an exponential rate. Each price bar increases in size and if it is an uptrend, the curve begins to look like the right hand side of a circle – as it nears the diameter. It stands to reason that the closer the market gets to vertical, the better the chance for a parabolic trade – since no market can go up forever.

For good examples in liquid markets, take a look at silver in the 1970s and in 2011, or the Nasdaq in 2011. The more vertical or parabolic the state of the market, the bigger the resulting price correction usually is. The reason for this is that the same traders and speculators that drive a market higher usually all sell at the same time causing the market to reverse significantly.

Here is a recent example of a stock going parabolic as a result of rampant speculation: Source:finviz.com

Taking profits

Entering into a parabolic move can be scary, since the market is at its most rampant. Adverse price moves are therefore common and your position is most likely to lose money at first.

However, it is important to wait. If you have entered into a true parabolic move you do not have to endure too much pain for too long. Indeed once the correction comes you are likely to see the market lose as much as 50% and you will have successfully burst your first bubble. It's important not to get too greedy though and you should aim to target no more than 20-30% profit.

Time frames

Generally, parabolic moves are best traded over longer time frames. Trying to identify parabolics in short-term charts such as 15-minute or 1-hour charts is a very dangerous strategy since price moves can go on for much longer periods. It is therefore best to seek out parabolic moves in monthly or weekly charts only. You should also try to look at the fundamentals to support your theory. In general, any analysis you can gather to support your trade helps you with the conviction you need to trade against the trend.

HOW TO USE THE AVERAGE TRUE RANGE

The average true range (ATR) indicator is a simple tool but is very useful in measuring volatility. It is another indicator that was developed by J. Welles Wilder and can be used on any market successfully.

Simply put, the ATR measures the price range of a stock or security – the higher the volatility of a security the higher the ATR.

The ATR is measured as the greatest of any of the following three metrics:

The current high minus the low;
The value of the current high minus the previous close;
The value of the current low minus the previous close.

Whichever is the highest of these three metrics is then represented as the average true range of the security. Typically, the number is then smoothed using a 14-day moving average.

Finding the average range of a security has a number of important implications that can help make better trading decisions.

Using the ATR outright to trade volatility

First of all, the ATR can be used as a trading signal in its own right. Let's say that you are watching a market for a number of days and you have noticed that volatility has dropped significantly from its historical average. Since low periods of volatility often precede explosive moves in either direction, you could wait for the ATR to increase and place a trade in the direction of the move. Crossovers can also be used. For example, placing a trade when the fast ATR (e.g. 14 period) crosses over a slower ATR (e.g. 100 period). This can be an effective breakout volatility strategy, joining the market as it really starts to move.

Using the ATR for profit targets

For day traders, knowing the average range of a security is extremely useful since it allows you to estimate how much profit potential there is in the market.

For example, there is no point looking for 150 pips of profit from a trade in GBP/USD, if the average true range for that market over the last 14 days is only 80 pips. You end up seeking unrealistic profits and are likely to lose money.

A better solution is to halve the 14-day ATR and use this as your profit target. In other words, after entering a trade in GBP/USD, you can give yourself a profit target of around 40 pips. This is a much safer way to trade.

Using the ATR as a filter

The average true range is also a good indicator to use for filtering out trades. Traders typically need volatility to make any money so if you have a system that generates lots of different signals, you can filter out those ones that are low in volatility by discarding those with a low ATR. Concentrating on markets with the highest ATRs mean you can trade the markets that are experiencing the most movement and therefore the most profit potential.

Conversely, looking for stocks with smaller ATRs means you might be able to find more stable and cheaper stocks.

SOME FINAL TIPS FOR TECHNICAL ANALYSIS TRADERS

As we have seen there are many ways to trade from the chart and it is a skill which takes years of practise to get right. The advantages of doing so, however, are great, since technical analysis trading is based solely on price moves. This means that chart traders often develop good instincts on the markets. An emphasis on price moves also means that technicians are able to develop better risk management systems.

Longer-term charts offer fewer whipsaws

A good thing to remember when trading from the chart is that charts on different time frames tend to have different characteristics. Typically, longer-term charts such as hourly charts or daily charts, have less noise, which means there are fewer whipsaws. 1-minute charts or tick charts, by comparison, provide lots of opportunities but many of them are false signals.

Know your indicator

Probably the biggest mistake that new traders make is to use an indicator without fully realizing how it works. Technical indicators can have thousands of settings and some work better than others. It's therefore imperative to read the documentation concerning the indicator in question and find out exactly how it works before applying it to the chart.

Combining indicators provides better signals

Improving the strength of a trading signal can be accomplished by combining indicators. Consider adding a moving average crossover signal to an RSI indicator, for example. This works best when the indicators complement each other and measure different things. But don't use too many indicators, since over complicated strategies do not work so well.

Not all indicators are the same

Most people know about the most popular indicators such as Bollinger Bands and moving averages, however, there are thousands more out there. The thing is, some are better than others. Many are based on little more than hunch, so always find indicators that are known to work well or try to create your own.

Realize patterns are subjective and have an exit plan

While some indicators provide objective signals such as moving average crossovers, some indicators are more subjective. Subjective patterns can be okay as long as you have an exit plan if the market goes against you, but they are not so easily incorporated into statistical testing so this should be considered.

Stick to what you know – same chart, same settings

There is no point in switching between different time frames when looking for a trade. There is always a possible trade if you look hard enough but it probably won't be the strongest.

Likewise, there is little use in switching between different markets or different settings on your indicator. You simply end up finding trades you have little confidence in. Stick to one time frame and one market and keep the same settings and you become a more consistent trader.

Crossovers are key

There is a reason why crossovers are used so extensively in technical analysis. They take place during market turning points and are mathematically set-up to offer the best entry points. So make sure to keep this in mind when looking at a chart.

CHAPTER 6:
TRADING SYSTEMS

WHY USE A TRADING SYSTEM?

Trading systems represent the best way to tackle the issue of emotions in trading and are used by many successful traders and hedge funds to great effect.

However, finding a trading system and implementing it is not as simple as it sounds and there are many things that need to be considered first.

Designing a system

The first thing to think about when designing a trading system concerns your personal trading goals. What do you hope to achieve and what sort of returns will you be happy with? What markets do you plan to trade?

You should be sure about what your beliefs are. Do you ascribe to a certain philosophy such as markets always follow trends or markets fluctuate around the mean?

If you can understand this (and your goals are not too unrealistic) you can begin to find a system that fits your criteria.

Perhaps you already have a strategy in your head, maybe using technical indicators, and you want to get it on paper and test it more scientifically.

Back-testing historical data

Once you have an idea of your strategy, the next step is to get hold of some historical data and some software for testing your system. There are plenty of trading platforms out there now that allow back-testing and plenty of resources on the Internet for finding historical data.

My trading platform of choice is Amibroker as it is affordable, fast and does everything I need. For historical data, one good site that I use is premiumdata.net.

Google and Yahoo provide decent and free end-of-day data, but it can sometimes have errors so be careful.

Testing a system requires a great deal of data in order to be able to validate it successfully and this varies depending on your time frame. If you are trading using end-of-day data then you should aim for at least five, preferably 10 years' worth of data. If you are trading intraday, then 12 months' tick data ought to be enough. Bear in mind, the shorter the time frame, the more the data costs.

The important thing now is to freeze the data over a certain time period. This time period will be used for testing the system and the rest will be reserved for out-of-sample testing.

In-sample, out-of-sample

Consider freezing around 2 or 3 years' worth of data and using this to test your trading ideas. Only when you are happy with the results can you then try testing it on the out-of-sample data. You should only ever do this once. The moment you start testing your system on the out-of-sample data it becomes contaminated and statistically invalid since you are using information from previous tests to inform your decisions on future data.

This is the most important part of testing a trading system, make sure you keep your in-sample and out-of-sample data separate at all times.

Diagnostic testing

Now you have your data set frozen, begin your analysis by running some very crude tests over the data. Keep a notepad by your side so you can make some notes on what you find. You don't want to forget the information that the tests tell you.

It's important to start with some very rough tests. You are looking for a system that stands up under different market conditions, so there is no point optimizing a system to work perfectly over a certain time period of data.

It's also a good idea, at this point, to decide on a metric by which to judge your system.

CAR/MDD (compounded annual return divided by maximum drawdown) is a good one, since it delivers the result that makes the most money while limiting losses.

Run your trading ideas over a very broad range of settings, from slowest to fastest. For example, if you are interested in a moving average crossover system, you may want to test moving average crossovers using EMAs from 5 days up to 300 days.

You'll quickly discover that your trading idea works best on certain ranges of settings. You can now disregard the settings that don't work as well and focus in on the settings that work the best.

Keep dialling in until you find a 'sweet spot' – where the system performs at its best.

Optimising parameters

You can fine tune your system further by optimising any number of different parameters – something that can be done easily now in most trading programs. Try testing different exit and entry ideas, use different stop losses and profit targets, and test different money management techniques or filters.

However, always remember: the more parameters there are, the more chance the system has of becoming curve-fit with the data. Each extra setting increases this chance exponentially. A robust trading system should therefore only have a few changeable parameters.

Keep fine tuning your system until you have a strategy that performs well over your data then test it once on out-of-sample data. If it performs nearly as well on your out-of-sample data as your in-sample data, you have a system that stands up to testing – congratulations.

Make sure it is robust by continuing to test it over other periods of out-of-sample data (walk forward testing) and over other markets.

You may also consider using Monte Carlo analysis to further test its statistical chances.

System designing is a tricky business, so the bottom line is to test your idea on as many different markets and time frames as possible. Only a system that works well across many different scenarios can be classed as reliable enough to trade in real life.

Curve-fit

Curve-fitting means developing a system that works almost perfectly on past data generating superior results. Curve-fitting must be avoided at all costs as curve-fit systems will have next to no chance of reproducing those results on future data.

It's important to stay completely unbiased when you run your tests. Let's say your in-sample data is 2006-2007 and your out-of-sample data is 2008-2009. You already know that there was a big crash in 2008 so you know what type of markets will make money during that period.

Make sure you test and validate your system objectively and on untested, independent data.

Looking into the future

Another mistake that you need to avoid is to make sure your system does not reference any future data. When programming, it can sometimes be easy to overlook certain things which can mean that your system could actually look into the future.

For example, if your system relies on a moving average crossover that is calculated using the close price, you must make sure your system does not enter positions on the open. This can easily happen during testing but is obviously not possible in the real world.

Thankfully, this is usually easy to spot as a system often produces extraordinary results when it looks into the future. Many programs, Amibroker included, are able to check for references to future data.

Paper trading

The whole purpose of designing a system is to predict what will happen in the future by studying the past. You must therefore test your system on clean, future data before you start trading real money and the best way to do that is to paper trade your system for a while once you are happy with it.

Of course, the future will never be known and many trading systems that worked in the past no longer work anymore.

You should therefore aim to constantly test your system as you go. If it starts performing differently to how it did in the past then there's a chance that it is broken. Indeed, there are steps that you can take to test whether the system is broken or not. For an in depth discussion of this, you can take a look at Dr Howard Bandy's book, Modelling Trading System Performance. Bandy suggests a number of metrics that you can look at to decide whether your system is still working.

Personality

It's also important to find a system that fits your trading personality since you need to be able to tolerate the swings in equity it produces. You don't want to design a system that you have trouble sticking to. For a system to work effectively, you need to follow every signal it produces so sticking to the system is crucial.

Aim to find a system that produces low drawdowns over different markets and time frames and you will be on your way.

MEASURING SYSTEM PERFORMANCE

Once you have a system, it is important to be able to analyze it properly so you can assess its ability to make future gains. Most of these metrics can be calculated by your trading platform.

The equity curve

The fastest and easiest way to measure a trading system is to eyeball its equity curve. If the equity line is erratic and looks like a rocky mountain face then this is probably an erratic system. The system may use any number of indicators but in truth, the results may be more or less random.

However, if the equity line is near perfectly straight and goes up almost in a straight diagonal line, then this system is probably too good to be true. Take a closer look to make sure it is not curve-fit and that it doesn't reference future data. And make sure it doesn't use an unsustainable position sizing strategy such as Martingale.

A desirable equity curve should be a fairly smooth upward sloping line that works over different market conditions and time frames.

CAR

CAR stands for compounded annual return and is delivered as a percentage. It shows how much the portfolio returns per year. A high CAR sure looks nice but it is not always the best metric to measure system performance since it does not take into account risk at all.

CAR/MDD

CAR/MDD is thus a better metric to measure system performance as it analyzes percentage annual growth divided by the maximum drawdown. (Maximum drawdown refers to the largest peak to peak decline in portfolio equity.)

Essentially, the higher the CAR/MDD score, the smoother the equity curve and the better the system.

Profit factor

Profit factor can be a good measure, since it divides the profit of winners by the loss of losers. It's a quick way to look at the chances of your system being profitable over time.

Risk-reward ratio

Risk-reward ratio can be measured by dividing the slope of the equity line by the standard error of the equity line. It's an important metric to be able to calculate the optimum position sizing for a system as we discussed in Chapter 3.

Sharpe ratio

Sharpe is a popular metric, developed by William Sharpe in 1966. It describes how much return you receive from the added volatility for holding a trade. Basically, the higher the Sharpe ratio, the better the system. However, Sharpe ratio has come under criticism for not recognising that upward volatility is more desirable than downward volatility.

K-Ratio

Another popular measure, K-Ratio examines the consistency of an asset's return over time. It generally does a good job of measuring risk versus return and involves running a linear regression on the equity curve.

GETTING STARTED ON YOUR TRADING SYSTEM

The best thing about designing a trading system is that if you know how to code you can put any idea you have in your head down on to paper and see if it would have worked in the real world. If you can't code, you can hire someone to do it for you. It's a really creative process and a lot of fun testing out your ideas.

But before we look at some system ideas, it's important to understand the preparation that I have put into each system.

Data

Each test in this chapter is run on historical data for stocks in the S&P 500 index spanning from August 1, 2000 to August 1, 2010. That's 10 years of data for 500 stocks which should be plenty to draw some decent conclusions. By fixing the data over these dates, we have left three years of out-of-sample data with which we can validate the findings at a later date. (By the way, I chose to start in August for no other reason than the fact other system developers nearly always start in January.)

Time frames

Each test is run on weekly end-of-day data unless otherwise indicated. Although some traders prefer trading daily, I find trading on a weekly basis tends to provide smoother results.

Risk

Each test is run on a portfolio of 10 positions. The starting capital is set at $10,000 which is then divided equally by the number of positions to give the position value per trade.

In other words, each position has an initial value of $1000. To get the number of shares simply divide $1000 by the share price.

This position size changes as the capital increases or decreases. For example, if capital drops down to $9000, each position has a value of $900. Trading like this means you can never go completely broke. It also allows the magic of compounding to take effect.

Commissions

For simplicity, commissions have been set at 0.2% per trade. 0.4% for a round trip (buy and sell).

Delisted stocks

Delisted securities are those stocks that have been taken off the exchange and should usually be included in back-testing. However, due to the difficulties of obtaining, referencing and including delisted stock data, delisted stocks have been left out of these tests. It is up to you to find a way to incorporate delisted data into your own analysis.

Important

The idea of including these tests is not to provide trading advice but rather to give some guidance as to how to start thinking about trading systems. As presented here, the tests are only rough guides and would usually benefit from extra work.

While every effort has been made to test these trading systems in a fair and accurate way, it is strongly advised not to trade any of these ideas without testing them rigorously in your own time.

Before investing any money make sure you have tested the system on out-of-sample data and used data that includes delisted securities.

TRADING SYSTEM 1: MOVING AVERAGE CROSSOVER (LONG ONLY)

We begin with a simple trend following system that buys a stock when the 10-week moving average crosses over the 18-week moving average and sells it when it crosses back under. The weekly moving average is calculated using the open price while entries and exits are initiated on the close.

The system has a compounded annual return (CAR) of 13.37% over the 10 years with a maximum drawdown of 47%. It entered into a total of 281 trades of which 49% were winners.

The payoff ratio (average win/average loss) is 1.76 while risk reward is 0.79.

Although the drawdown is large, this system produces an adequate return for some.

Net Profit	CAR	RAR	Max. Sys % Drawdown	Recovery Factor	CAR/MDD
25036.48	13.37	59.47	-47.19	1.23	0.28
Profit Factor	Payoff Ratio	RRR	# Trades	Avg Bars Held	% Winners
1.7	1.76	0.79	281	19.36	49.11

Source: Amibroker

181

TRADING SYSTEM 2: FOUR WEEKS UP IN A ROW (LONG ONLY)

Another long only trend following system, this one enters a position after a stock has opened higher 4 weeks in a row and sells when the 10-week EMA crosses under the 15-week EMA. The idea is similar to that of the three white soldiers candlestick pattern where several weeks up in a row signifies strength in the stock. As you can see, the system worked well for a time but has not been able to recover its 2007 peak.

Net Profit	CAR	RAR	Max. Sys % Drawdown	Recovery Factor	CAR/MDD
27720.71	14.21	79.72	-48.65	1.07	0.29
Profit Factor	Payoff Ratio	RRR	# Trades	Avg Bars Held	% Winners
1.75	1.55	0.55	198	27.51	53.03

Source: Amibroker

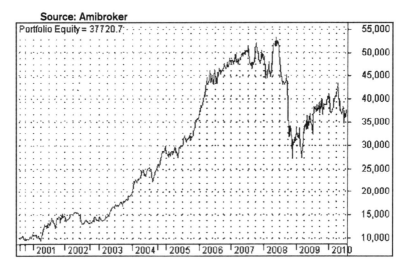

TRADING SYSTEM 3: TRADING THE NOISE (LONG ONLY)

Trading trends is easier when markets move smoothly, without noise. In this system, noise in the market is calculated as:

$$N = (Low/Open) + (Close/High) + (Open/High) + (Low/Close)$$

A 5-week moving average is then taken of the noise (N) and a position is entered when N is above 3.8. (This indicates less noise and a smoother trend.)

A sell order is initiated when N drops back below 3.64 – indicating more noise and more volatile trading conditions.

Noise is calculated using the previous week's data and positions are entered on the close.

Net Profit	CAR	RAR	Max. Sys % Drawdown	Recovery Factor	CAR/MDD
62843.67	21.99	42.5	-39.54	1.66	0.56
Profit Factor	Payoff Ratio	RRR	# Trades	Avg Bars Held	% Winners
6.69	6.25	1.01	29	179.55	51.72

Source: Amibroker

183

TRADING SYSTEM 4:TRADING THE NOISE PLUS SHORTS

This is the same as trading system 3 but with additional shorts. Short positions are entered when the noise drops below 3.64 and covered when the noise moves above 3.8 (in other words, the reverse signal to long positions). Notice how adding shorts increases returns and also reduces drawdowns, resulting in a smoother equity curve. In 10 years, the system had only one down year (2008).

Net Profit	CAR	RAR	Max. Sys % Drawdown	Recovery Factor	CAR/MDD
75333.71	23.93	44.03	-38.25	2.94	0.63
Profit Factor	**Payoff Ratio**	**RRR**	**# Trades**	**Avg Bars Held**	**% Winners**
11.28	5.43	1.15	40	132.85	67.5

Source: Amibroker

TRADING SYSTEM 5: TRADING GRADIENTS (LONG ONLY)

This is a mean reversion strategy using daily data and relies on a simple indicator. The formula for the indicator measures the slope between the two most recent points on a 24 period EMA:

GRA = EMA(Open,24) / Yesterday's (EMA(Open,24),-1)

Using this formula, it is easy to see which stocks are dropping or rising the fastest. The aim is then to find stocks that have dropped so much that their slope is almost vertical.

A buy position is initiated whenever a stock's GRA drops below 0.98. This indicates the stock is significantly oversold. When the GRA moves past 1.02, the position is closed. The system uses open prices to calculate the slope and positions are entered on the weekly close.

Net Profit	CAR	RAR	Max. Sys % Drawdown	Recovery Factor	CAR/MDD
36967.48	16.73	42.11	-47.47	1.35	0.35
Profit Factor	Payoff Ratio	RRR	# Trades	Avg Bars Held	% Winners
4.85	3.34	0.80	49	612	59.18

Source: Amibroker

185

TRADING SYSTEM 6: DOLLAR COST AVERAGING

DCA was talked about in Chapter 2 and is more of an investment strategy. As you can see it does produce OK returns.

The idea is to invest $1000 each month in a portfolio of stocks or ETFs without ever selling. When the market is down you get more for your money, while when the market is up you're unable to buy as much. Over the long-term, profits smooth out, although the drawdown in 2008 was high.

Net Profit	CAR	RAR	Max. Sys % Drawdown	Recovery Factor	CAR/MDD
159577.93	8.83	34.04	-47.11	1.28	0.19
Profit Factor	Payoff Ratio	RRR	# Trades	Avg Bars Held	% Winners
15.1	6.47	0.58	10	122	70

Source: Amibroker

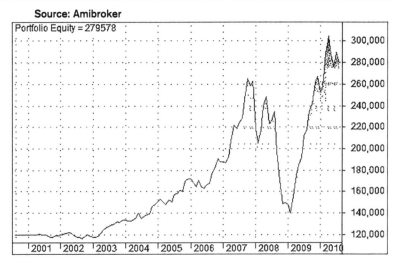

TRADING SYSTEM 7: DONCHIAN STYLE BREAKOUT

This is similar to the breakout strategy made famous by Richard Donchian, a version of which was used successfully by the turtle traders.

The system enters a position on the open after a 55-week high and sells on the open after a 20-week low. Shorts are entered after a 75-week low and covered after a 30-week high.

However, I have limited short positions to a maximum of 5 (out of 10). (Shorts do not seem to fare so well when back-testing stocks.)

Net Profit	CAR	RAR	Max. Sys % Drawdown	Recovery Factor	CAR/MDD
30320.86	14.97	44.37	-24.57	3.70	0.61
Profit Factor	Payoff Ratio	RRR	# Trades	Avg Bars Held	% Winners
2.41	3.62	0.83	135	39	40

Source: Amibroker

187

TRADING SYSTEM 8: BREAKOUT WITH EMA CONFIRMATION

This is the same system as trading system 7 but it uses an EMA crossover as a confirmation filter. In this case, longs are entered on a breakout but only if the 5-week EMA is above the 20-week EMA. Similarly, shorts are entered only if the 50 week EMA is below the 40 week EMA.

Filters can often be good for systems that produce a lot of signals. However, always be aware that each filter you introduce increases the complexity of the system and the likelihood it is curve-fit.

Net Profit	CAR	RAR	Max. Sys % Drawdown	Recovery Factor	CAR/MDD
40074.60	17.49	45.17	-26.52	2.62	0.66
Profit Factor	Payoff Ratio	RRR	# Trades	Avg Bars Held	% Winners
2.44	3.49	0.87	124	43	41.13

Source: Amibroker

188

TRADING SYSTEM 9: TREND FOLLOWING WITH THE TEMA

Another trend following system, this time utilizing the faster moving TEMA. The system goes long when the 80-week TEMA crosses over the 95-week TEMA and goes short when the opposite occurs.

Net Profit	CAR	RAR	Max. Sys % Drawdown	Recovery Factor	CAR/MDD
69583.18	23.07	59.79	-28.78	2.77	0.8
Profit Factor	Payoff Ratio	RRR	# Trades	Avg Bars Held	% Winners
2.94	2.6	1.04	81	66.27	53.09

Source: Amibroker

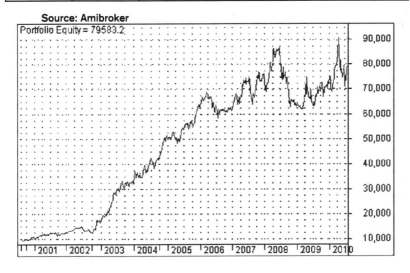

189

TRADING SYSTEM 10: BULL/BEAR FEAR

This system attempts to identify periods of bullishness or bearishness in the market by using the following calculation:

BullFear = (Highest High Value (High,n) – Lowest Low Value (High,n))/2 + Lowest Low Value (High,n)

BearFear = (HHV(Low,n) – LLV(Low,n))/2 + LLV(Low,n)

The system then goes long when the closing price crosses bull fear and goes short when bear fear crosses under the close.

In addition, the system uses an average directional index filter (10) to filter trades. It enters positions on the next open.

Since the system performs with relatively low drawdowns, risk was doubled for this test.

Thanks to Marek Choplek for the code.

Net Profit	CAR	RAR	Max. Sys % Drawdown	Recovery Factor	CAR/MDD
75030.79	23.89	55.29	-32.29	3.61	0.74

Profit Factor	Payoff Ratio	RRR	# Trades	Avg Bars Held	% Winners
1.49	2.06	1.19	393	14.4	41.98

Source: Amibroker

190

TRADING SYSTEM 11: SIMPLE RSI WITH EQUITY CURVE FILTER (DAILY)

This is a simple relative strength indicator (RSI) trading strategy combined with an equity curve filter.

RSI is normally used for reversion strategies but I found by changing the settings slightly it can follow trends too.

Profits tend to come in runs when trading, so this system uses the equity curve to scale back positions during losing streaks and increase size during winning streaks.

This system was tested on daily data and buys when the 14-day RSI crosses 70. It exits when the RSI crosses under 30 and the reverse is true for shorts. Since RSI is calculated using the closing price, this model trades on the next day's open. Risk was increased by a factor of 2 in order to improve returns.

Net Profit	CAR	RAR	Max. Sys % Drawdown	Recovery Factor	CAR/MDD
43351.4	18.23	40.19	-37.74	2.11	0.48
Profit Factor	Payoff Ratio	RRR	# Trades	Avg Bars Held	% Winners
1.82	2.13	0.72	154	159.18	46.1

Source: Amibroker

191

TRADING SYSTEM 12: THE RANGE INDICATOR (TRI)

The range indicator system (TRI) was developed by Jack L. Weinberg and was presented in Stocks & Commodities magazine.

TRI uses the intraday range divided by today's close, minus yesterdays close. This information is used to build a stochastic in order to show market direction.

However, I adapted this system to work on weekly data.

A buy order is entered on the open when TRI is lower than 8. It sells when TRI is greater than 70.

Shorts are entered when TRI is greater than 8 and covered when TRI is lower than 10.

Thanks to Marek Chlopek for the code.

Net Profit	CAR	RAR	Max. Sys % Drawdown	Recovery Factor	CAR/MDD
62864.27	21.99	137.9	-40.44	2.55	0.54
Profit Factor	Payoff Ratio	RRR	# Trades	Avg Bars Held	% Winners
2.54	1.61	0.94	173	31.61	61.27

Source: Amibroker

TRADING SYSTEM 13: VOLATILITY BREAKOUT WITH BOLLINGER BANDS AND CHANDE VPI

This system buys the market on the close when the open price is higher than the top Bollinger Band (15.2). It sells when the open price is lower than the bottom Bollinger Band. The reverse occurs for shorts.

In addition, the system use a volatility filter called VPI, which was developed by Tushar Chande. VPI attempts to find the most explosive stocks and trades are taken when VPI is greater than 10.

Net Profit	CAR	RAR	Max. Sys % Drawdown	Recovery Factor	CAR/MDD
87850.6	25.64	61.86	-36.97	3.67	0.69
Profit Factor	Payoff Ratio	RRR	# Trades	Avg Bars Held	% Winners
2.48	2.57	0.82	112	46.01	49.11

Source: Amibroker

193

TRADING SYSTEM 14: TRADING THE GAP (LONG ONLY)

Whenever a gap occurs, it usually means the majority of traders have gone to one side of the market, and often, the market springs back and fills in the gap.

This is a long only mean reversion system that buys a stock when it opens 1% lower than the previous week's low. It therefore seeks to capture profits where a stock has opened much lower than expected and exits the position at the end of the week. Since only one position is allowed per week, risk was increased to improve returns.

This system relies on having a method to place entries precisely on the open such as an automated program.

Net Profit	CAR	RAR	Max. Sys % Drawdown	Recovery Factor	CAR/MDD
624372.16	51.49	130.56	-36.94	1.69	1.39
Profit Factor	Payoff Ratio	RRR	# Trades	Avg Bars Held	% Winners
1.41	1.33	0.8	231	2.02	51.52

Source: Amibroker

TRADING SYSTEM 15: RSI WITH THE VIX (DAILY, LONG ONLY)

The VIX, volatility index is provided by the Chicago Board Options Exchange and is a good guide for measuring fear in the market. It can therefore be used as a suitable filter for taking or not taking trades.

In this case, longs are only taken if the RSI crosses 70 and the VIX index is in a downtrend – signalling decreasing volatility in the broader market.

Trades are closed when the RSI crosses under 30.

This is a long only, end of day system that might benefit from incorporating shorts and tinkering with risk.

Net Profit	CAR	RAR	Max. Sys % Drawdown	Recovery Factor	CAR/MDD
88721.52	25.73	74.55	-44.9	2.33	0.57
Profit Factor	Payoff Ratio	RRR	# Trades	Avg Bars Held	% Winners
3.95	4.29	0.9	121	192.69	47.93

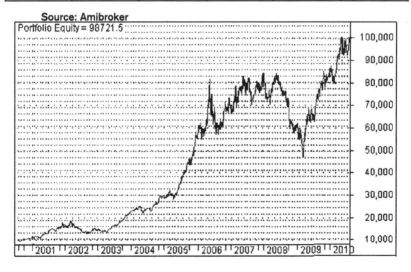

Source: Amibroker

TRADING SYSTEM 16: TRADING THE TED SPREAD (DAILY)

The TED spread is calculated as the difference between the 3-month LIBOR rate and the 3-month T-Bill rate and is another good indicator of fear in the market.

The TED spread normally widens during periods of economic stress as was seen in the 2008 crisis where it became an indicator synonymous with the crash.

This system goes long when a stock opens at its highest open for 110 days. It closes the position when it opens at its lowest of 80 days. The reverse is true for short positions.

It is therefore a simple breakout formula. However it only goes long if the TED spread is lower than 1. It only goes short if the TED spread is greater than 1.

Net Profit	CAR	RAR	Max. Sys % Drawdown	Recovery Factor	CAR/MDD
86750.04	25.48	73.04	-26.19	4.47	0.97
Profit Factor	Payoff Ratio	RRR	# Trades	Avg Bars Held	% Winners
3.35	3.2	1.41	131	184.8	51.15

Source: Amibroker

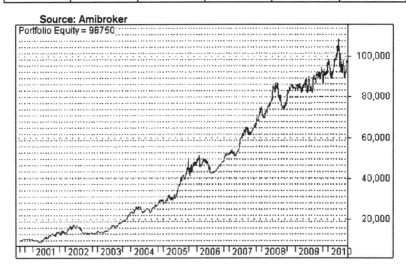

196

TRADING SYSTEM 17: SIMPLE MACD WITH EMA FILTER

This system goes long or short when the MACD indicator crosses over its signal. The MACD used in this test was found to work best with the settings (12, 25, 17). It works well but sometimes enters trades in stocks that are going in the wrong direction.

The system was therefore improved by using the gradient of an EMA to filter out trades. This is a weekly system.

Net Profit	CAR	RAR	Max. Sys % Drawdown	Recovery Factor	CAR/MDD
52958.26	20.22	98.53	-28.26	2.94	0.72
Profit Factor	Payoff Ratio	RRR	# Trades	Avg Bars Held	% Winners
1.93	2.9	0.94	323	12.24	39.94

Source: Amibroker

197

TRADING SYSTEM 18: CHERRY PICKING PENNY STOCKS WITH EMA CROSSOVER

This system takes a slightly different approach.

Since the EMA crossover used results in many signals on different stocks, it is necessary to cherry pick which of those signals to take.

It uses a simple ATR calculation so that those with small ATRs are then preferred to those with higher ATR's. It therefore prefers smaller stocks over larger ones. Since penny stocks can provide explosive growth opportunities this may work well on another watch list, for example the S&P small cap index.

The system is weekly and trades on the close.

Net Profit	CAR	RAR	Max. Sys % Drawdown	Recovery Factor	CAR/MDD
132376.9	30.45	54.32	-30.18	3.18	1.01
Profit Factor	Payoff Ratio	RRR	# Trades	Avg Bars Held	% Winners
3.66	5.91	0.89	115	46.89	38.26

Source: Amibroker

198

TRADING SYSTEM 19: USING THE COMMITMENT OF TRADERS REPORT

This is essentially a trend following system. It goes long on a stock when the 10-week EMA crosses over the 30-week EMA and goes short when the reverse occurs. It then uses the Commitment of Traders (COT) report as a filter.

The COT report measures weekly open positions for commercial, non-commercial and retail participants for the Dow Jones Industrial Average future. I found that when commercial traders increase their short positions in the index in comparison to non-commercial traders, it is often a good time to buy. Conversely, when non-commercial traders increase their shorts, it is usually a time to sell.

Net Profit	CAR	RAR	Max. Sys % Drawdown	Recovery Factor	CAR/MDD
36401.69	16.6	35.73	-19.56	4.05	0.85
Profit Factor	Payoff Ratio	RRR	# Trades	Avg Bars Held	% Winners
6.09	6.27	1.07	67	77.42	49.25

Source: Amibroker

TRADING SYSTEM 20: FINDING CHEAP STOCKS WITH LINEAR REGRESSION AND AVERAGE TRUE RANGE

The linear regression indicator plots the end points of series of linear regression lines that are drawn over consecutive days. It is good for finding trends, but erratic unless the data is smoothed using moving averages.

This system, therefore, goes long on a stock when the 15-week moving average of the 5 period linear regression indicator crosses over the 65-week moving average of the 5 period indicator. It goes short when the opposite occurs.

The system then uses the average true range to sort between different signals. Thus, the system favors cheap stocks with low ATRs. A minimum price of $1 is set so as not to trade inefficient penny stocks.

Net Profit	CAR	RAR	Max. Sys % Drawdown	Recovery Factor	CAR/MDD
53997.02	20.42	49.01	-21.21	4.54	0.96
Profit Factor	Payoff Ratio	RRR	# Trades	Avg Bars Held	% Winners
5.29	4.75	1.2	93	57.54	52.69

Source: Amibroker

200

CHAPTER 7:
RESOURCES AND BONUS MATERIAL

RESOURCES AND LINKS

Chapter 1: Trading fundamentals

Online

PIMCO, www.pimco.com

Print

Buffet, Mary and David Clark. (1999). Buffetology. Scribner.

Bulkowski, Thomas N. (2013). Fundamental Analysis and Position Trading. John Wiley & Sons.

Hayes, Timothy. (2000). The Research Driven Investor: How to Use Information, Data and Analysis for Investment Success. McGraw-Hill.

Moss, David A. (2007). Concise Guide to Macroeconomics: What Managers, Executives, and Students Need to Know. Harvard Business Review Press.

Rogers, Jim. (2004). Adventure Capitalist: The Ultimate Road Trip. Random House Trade.

Rogers, Jim. (2007). Hot Commodities: How Anyone Can Invest Profitably in the World's Best Market. John Wiley & Sons.

Rogers, Jim. (2013). Street Smarts: Adventures on the Road and in the Markets. Crown Publishing Group.

Schroeder, Alice. (2009). The Snowball: Warren Buffett and the Business of Life. Bloomsbury Publishing.

Soros, Geroge. (2003). The Alchemy of Finance: Reading the Mind of the Market. John Wiley & Sons.

Soros, George. (1995). Soros on Soros: Staying Ahead of the Curve. John Wiley & Sons.

Chapter 2: Timing

Online

Barrons, www.barrons.com

COT report, www.cftc.gov

Commodity Yearbook, www.crbyearbook.com

InvestExcel, www.investexcel.net

Investors Intelligence, www.investorsintelligence.com

Momentum investing white paper, www.aqrindex.com

Oanda, www.oanda.com

Print

Arnold, Glen. (2011). Financial Times Guide to the Financial Markets. Financial Times.

Fergus, Naill. (2012). The Ascent of Money: A Financial History of the World. Penguin.

Fisher, Philip A. (1996). Common Stocks and Uncommon Profits and Other Writings. John Wiley & Sons.

Fridson, Martin S. and Fernando Alvarez. (2011). Financial Statement Analysis: A Practitioner's Guide. John Wiley & Sons.

Graham, Benjamin. (2005). The Intelligent Investor. HarperBusiness.

Graham, Benjamin. (2002). Security Analysis. McGraw-Hill.

Greenblatt, Joel. (2010). The Little Book That Still Beats the Market. John Wiley & Sons.

Makoujy, Rick. (2010). How to Read a Balance Sheet: The Bottom Line on What You Need to Know about Cash Flow, Assets, Debt, Equity, Profit...and How It all Comes Together. McGraw-Hill.

Mckenzie, Wendy. (2003). Financial Times Guide to Using and

Interpreting Company Accounts. Financial Times.

O'Neil, William J. (2009). How to Make Money in Stocks: A Winning System in Good Time or Bad. McGraw-Hill.

Schannep, Jack. (2008). Dow Theory for the 21st Century. John Wiley & Sons.

Shiller, Robert. (2006). Irrational Exuberance. Broadway Business.

Skonieczny, Mariusz. (2012). The Basics of Understanding Financial Statements. Investment Publishing.

Chapter 3: Risk and Psychology

Online

Ed Seykota, www.seykota.com/tribe

Print

Akerlof, George and Robert Shiller. (2010). Animal Spirits: How Human Psychology Drives the Economy, and Why It Matters for Global Capitalism. Princeton University Press.

Kelly Formula: A New Interpretation of Information Rate. Bell System Technical Journal. Volume 35: 917-926.

Chen, Wai-Yee. (2013). Neuroinvesting: Build a New Investing Brain. Wiley.

Hull, John. (2012). Risk Management and Financial Institutions. Wiley.

Kindelberger, Charles. (2011). Manias, Panics, and Crashes: A History of Financial Crises. Palgrave Macmillan.

Mackay, Charles. (2013). Extraordinary Popular Delusions and the Madness of Crowds. Createspace.

Mandelbrot, Benoit and Richard L. Hudson. (2005). The Misbehavior of Markets: A Fractal View of Financial Turbulence. Basic Books.

Tharp, Van. (2006). Trade Your Way to Financial Freedom. McGraw-Hill.

Vince, Ralph. (1995). The New Money Management: A Framework for Asset Allocation. John Wiley & Sons.

Chapter 4: Trading tips

Online

MetaTrader, www.metatrader.com

Tradency, www.tradency.com

ZuluTrade, www.zulutrade.com

Print

Camillo, Chris. (2012). Laughing at Wall Street: How I Beat the Pros at Investing (by Reading Tabloids, Shopping at the Mall, and Connecting on Facebook) and How You Can, Too. St. Martin's Griffin.

Schiff, Peter. (2010). The Little Book of Bull Moves, Updated and Expanded: How to Keep Your Portfolio Up When the Market Is Up, Down, or Sideways. John Wiley & Sons.

Schiff, Peter. (2012). The Real Crash: America's Coming Bankruptcy — How to Save Yourself and Your Country. St Martin's Press.

Schwager, Jack D. (2012). Market Wizards. John Wiley & Sons.

Shon, John and Ping Zhou. (2011). Trading on Corporate Earnings News: Profiting from Targeted, Short-Term Options Positions. Financial Times/ Prentice Hill.

Staley, Kathryn. (1997). The Art of Short Selling. John Wiley & Sons.

Turk, James and John Rubino. (2004). The Coming Collapse of the Dollar and How to Profit from It: Make a Fortune by Investing in Gold and Other Hard Assets. Currency.

Chapter 5: Technical analysis

Online

John Bollinger, www.bollingerbands.com

Stocks & Commodities Magazine, www.traders.com

Print

Chande, Tushar. (2001). Beyond Technical Analysis: How to Develop and Implement a Winning Trading System. John Wiley & Sons.

Coulling, Anna. (2013). A Complete Guide to Volume Price Analysis. Anna Coulling.

Edwards, Robert D., John Magee and W. H. C. Bassetti. (2013). Technical Analysis of Stock Trends. CRC Press.

Link, Marcel. (2003). High Probability Trading: Take the Steps to Become a Successful Trader. McGraw-Hill.

Murphy, John J. (1999). Technical Analysis of the Financial Markets: A Comprehensive Guide to Trading Methods and Applications. Prentice Hall Press.

Nison, Steve. (2003). Japanese Candlestick Charting Techniques. Wiley.

Chapter 6: Trading systems

Online

Amibroker, www.amibroker.com

Trading Markets, www.tradingmarkets.com

Print

Bandy, Howard B. (2013). Mean Reversion Trading Systems. Blue Owl Press.

Bandy, Howard B. (2011). Modelling System Performance. Blue Owl Press.

Bandy, Howard B. (2007). Quantitative Trading Systems. Blue Owl Press.

Fitschen, Keith. (2013). Building Reliable Trading Systems: Tradable Strategies That Perform As They Backtest and Meet Your Risk-Reward Goals. John Wiley & Sons.

Chan, Ernie. (2013). Algorithmic Trading: Winning Strategies and Their Rationale. John Wiley & Sons.

Covel, Michael. (2009). The Complete Turtle Trader. HarperBusiness.

Covel, Michael. (2009). Trend Following: Learn to Make Millions in Up or Down Markets Trend Following. Financial Times/ Prentice Hall.

Kaufman, Perry J. (2013). Trading Systems and Methods. John Wiley & Sons.

Williams, Justine Gregory and Bill M. Williams. (2004). Trading Chaos: Maximize Profits with Proven Technical Techniques. John Wiley & Sons.

Miscellaneous

Broker websites

Barclays Stockbrokers, www.barclaysstockbrokers.co.uk

Forex Capital Markets, www.fxcm.com

E*Trade, www.etrade.com

IG Group, www.igmarkets.com

Interactive Brokers, www.interactivebrokers.com

Scottrade, www.scottrade.com

ChoiceTrade, www.choicetrade.com

Oanda, www.oanda.com

R. J. O' Brien, www.rjobrien.co.uk

TD Ameritrade, www.tdameritrade.com

TradeMonster, www.trademonster.com

Central bank websites

Bank of England, www.boe.gov.uk

European Central Bank, www.ecb.gov

Federal Reserve Bank, www.fed.gov.us

Economic data websites

Econ Data, www.econdata.net

Economagic, www.economagic.com

Finviz, www.finviz.com

Trading Economics, www.tradingeconomics.com

Wall Street Courier, www.wallstreetcourier.com

Rating agencies

Fitch, www.fitch.com

Moody's, www.moodys.com

Standard & Poor's, www.sandp.com

Stock exchange websites

ASE, www.asx.com.au

CBOE, www.cboe.com

CBOT, www.cbot.com

Euronext, www.euronext.com

LSE, www.lse.com

Nasdaq, www.nasdaq.com

NYSE, www.nyse.com

S&P, www.sandp.com

Historical data

AN Futures, www.anfutures.com

CSI Data, www.csidata.com

EOD Data, www.eoddata.com

Forex Tester, www.forextester.com

Google Finance, www.google.com

MSN Money, www.money.msn.com

Norgate Premium Data, www.premiumdata.net

Pinnacle Data, www.pinnacledata.com

Yahoo! Finance, www.finance.yahoo.com

Real time data and news

Bloomberg, www.bloomberg.com

CNBC, www.cnbc.com

CNN, www.cnn.com

CQG, www.cqg.com

eSignal, www.esignal.com

Interactive Brokers, www.interactivebrokers.com

Market Watch, www.marketwatch.com

Reuters, www.reuters.com

Online market comment/opinion

The Economist, www.economist.com

Financial Times, www.ft.com

Investors Chronicle, www.ic.co.uk

Hussman Funds, www.hussmanfunds.com

Money and Markets, www.moneyandmarkets.com

Seeking Alpha, www.seekingalpha.com

Wall Street Journal, www.wsj.com

Zero Hedge, www.zerohedge.com

Trading classics (print)

Faith, Curtis. (2007). Way of the Turtle. McGraw-Hill Professional.

Lewis, Michael. (2011). The Big Short. Penguin.

Livemore, Jesse. (2008). Reminiscences of a Stock Operator. John Wiley & Sons.

BEST OF THE BLOG AND BONUS MATERIAL

When writing this book, there were some things that I wanted to include but could not find the right place for in the main chapters. I have therefore included some extra words of wisdom over the following pages. Some of this was written fresh and some was taken directly from my blog at www.jbmarwood.com

INVESTMENT SCAMS TO AVOID

Every year, thousands of ordinary people succumb to the allure of an investment that is just too tempting to pass up. But be warned, if something seems too good to be true, in the investment world, it undoubtedly is. Following is a list of the most common scams which you should try to avoid at all costs:

Ponzi

The Ponzi scheme is a century-old swindle that involves paying the returns of investors using other investors' money. Of course, the Ponzi scheme was brought to light memorably in 2009 when it was revealed Bernie Madoff had elicited the biggest fraud in US history. Investors at the time, said they had been persuaded by the high returns of the fund and the fact it had never had a down year – a clear signal of something 'too good to be true'. If you find something that produces extraordinary returns with very little risk, always treat it with a grain of salt. Madoff is now serving 150 years in prison.

Boiler room

Boiler rooms operate by cold-calling ordinary people and trying to persuade them to buy the next hot investment. Typically, the broker tries to sell a stock (often a foreign company) that does not even exist. The company of course supplies a mass of professional-looking documentation and the salesmen uses his spiel to get you to buy into the stock. But it's fake, and if you fall for the trap there's little chance of seeing your money again. As I have shown in this book, it's best to do your own homework before you invest in anything and never consider falling for a sales pitch over the telephone.

Investment seminars

While some investment seminars are worth their salt, many of them (usually the free ones) are nothing more than a showcase to get people through the doors and then persuade them to invest further in the company. Also big in the real estate business, these companies often offer discount deals for further education or make commissions off future purchases. The best advice is to do your homework before you go and seek professional advice before committing any cash.

Day trading systems

While some trading systems work very well, the vast majority sold on the Web are scams or old systems that no longer work anymore. A con artist with an interest in finance has no trouble in formulating a system that appears to work perfectly over historical data, but when put over real time data, it will invariably fail.

Think about it. Why would anyone want to sell a day trading system that claims to make over 100% per annum for only $50-400?

The newsletter scam

The newsletter scam starts by an enterprising swindler sending out a thousand newsletters to a thousand clients. In half of them, the swindler gives advice to buy a stock, while in the other half he recommends to sell. Since half of his thousand clients received the right recommendation, the swindler then targets these people and sends out another 500 newsletters to only these clients. The scam is repeated until eventually there are around 10-20 clients who have received a sequence of stock picks, all of which have made money. The swindler then uses this new founded reputation to convince the client to subscribe to the paid for version of the newsletter.

In the investment game, it pays to be vigilant at all times.

TYPES OF ORDERS

If you are relatively new to trading you may know how to initiate a simple buy and sell trade with your favorite broker. But you may be unaware that there are several different ways to enter your trades, called order types. Depending upon what you want to do, it is useful to know the wide range of orders that are available.

Market order

A market order is probably the most common entry. It is used to enter the market at the best available price. In other words, if EUR/USD is trading with an ask price of 1.3280 and you put in a market order, you buy the currency at 1.3280 – all well and good.

The only time to be weary of using a market order is during illiquid markets. For example, say that you put in a market order to buy the open on EUR/USD. If the market is particularly volatile, it's possible for EUR/USD to gap up on the open and your best available price could be higher than what you were expecting.

Limit order

A limit order entry is placed when you want to buy markets above or below the current price.

So, if EUR/USD is trading at 1.3280 and you want to buy it at 1.327, you use a limit order placed below the market. Generally, you use a limit order when you want to enter at a better level.

Stop order

A stop order can be used to enter the market at a level higher or lower than it is now without having to wait around for the market to actually hit the price.

For example, say you want to buy EUR/USD when it breaks out past 1.3290. You can simply place a stop order to enter the market when the price touches 1.3291.

Stop loss

The stop loss order is used to close your trades and is the best way to protect your capital. It is a secure way of making sure that you can't lose anymore than a specified amount if your trade goes against you.

For example, if you have bought EUR/USD at 1.3280, you can put a stop loss in at 1.3260, meaning your loss is limited to only 20 pips.

The only way you could lose more than this is if the market gaps below your stop, at which time your stop is filled at the next best available price. This happens very rarely.

Trailing stop

The trailing stop order is a useful order for tracking the market when you don't want to spend your whole time watching the screen. You can enter a trailing stop order at a specific level away from the market and the stop then follows your trade up, or down, as it goes, thereby locking in a certain amount of profit.

For example, let's say you bought EUR/USD at 1.3280 and place your trailing stop 10 pips away. Supposing EUR/USD advances to 1.3300, your trailing stop moves up 20 pips to the 1.3290 level and you will have already locked in 10 pips profit.

Good 'til cancelled

The good 'til cancelled (GTC) order is used by traders who do not want their orders to be cancelled at the end of the trading session or because of any other reason. A GTC order, therefore, stays open in the markets indefinitely, meaning it is a trader's responsibility to be aware of the order at all times.

Good for the day

Unlike a GTC order, a good for the day (GFD) order stays open only until the end of the trading day. This means you can go to bed knowing you haven't left any running orders in the markets. However, since forex is traded 24 hours, the exact time of the end of the day may differ between brokers, so it pays to check first.

One cancels the other

This order is a useful entry strategy, particularly if you are using a volatility strategy or trading a news release.

Simply, a one cancels the other (OCO) order involves placing one order above the market and one below. When one order is touched and put into action, the other one is closed, so that only one position is entered into the market.

One useful application for this is when trading the news. Non-farm payrolls, for example, can often lead to big spikes in price in either direction. You could therefore place an OCO above or below the market just before the figure comes out. You are then guaranteed to enter a position in the direction of the market, while automatically closing the other order that is not touched.

One triggers the other

Similar to the OCO, the one triggers the other order is useful for when you aren't able to watch the markets 24/7. Using this order, you can set an entry order, target price as well as a stop price all at once, with the stop and target orders only becoming active if the entry order is entered.

For example, let's say that you want to buy EUR/USD if it touches 1.34. You also want to take profit at 1.345 and to put in a stop at 1.32. Well, by using a one triggers the other order, you can enter your position at 1.34 and the stop and profit orders only come into play once your entry order at 1.34 is opened.

HOW TO TAKE ADVANTAGE OF THE CARRY TRADE

The carry trade is often referred to in forex circles. It is a technique smart traders use to profit, not just from movement in a currency but from the interest rate differential between two countries. Countries that have higher interest rates offer more return on your money than those with lower rates, just like depositing money in a foreign bank offers a different return.

Essentially then, a carry trade involves borrowing money in a low interest rate account and investing it in a higher rate account and pocketing the difference.

And since spot forex markets accrue interest daily, it is possible to use the carry trade strategy every day.

One good example of a popular carry trade is AUD/JPY

Interest rates in Japan have been held at close to zero for years now in order to stimulate economic growth, while in Australia, rates are currently at 2.5%.

The interest rate differential is therefore 2.4% (2.5%–0.1%).

In other words, if you buy AUD/JPY, you accrue 2.4% in interest on your money and if you use leverage you can increase that return significantly over a year (with additional risk). If the currency also appreciates in that time, like it has done in AUD/JPY, then you achieve even greater gains.

How to play the carry trade

The best way to play the carry trade therefore is to find a high yielding currency pair that is also likely to appreciate as time goes on. (A 2% interest rate differential is going to be meaningless if the currency you've bought drops by 10%).

Generally, a country with good economic prospects sees its currency appreciate more than one that is not doing so well or has poor demographics. You can also look at the interest rate outlooks for both countries. If for example, you foresee Australia dropping rates, and Japan raising rates, your interest rate differential will fall. It will probably lead to a drop in the currency pair itself too.

When the carry trade works

As you can see, if you play the carry trade correctly, you can achieve a double whammy – higher interest on your investment as well as capital gains from your trade.

However, there are certain environments when the carry trade becomes ineffective.

During periods of market stress, there is usually an unwinding of the carry trade. In this instance, traders flock to traditional safe-haven currencies that offer low rates of return. It's therefore best to use the carry trade when most traders are optimistic about future returns.

WHAT IS THE EFFECT OF HOT MONEY ON THE ECONOMY?

Any investment denominated in a foreign currency can technically be referred to as hot money since it involves the transfer of capital from one country to another.

Typically, though, the term hot money has come to be known as the practice of moving money into another country in order to take advantage of interest rate differences or anticipated shifts in exchange rates. Such flows can have positive effects on an economy since they can boost a country's GDP and help to stimulate economic growth. However, when flows are only made for a short amount of time by speculators seeking to make a quick profit, negative implications can arise.

Currently, most hot money flows from developed countries into emerging markets and a large percentage of hot money at the moment ends up in China. Since China is growing at such an impressive rate, investments over there typically yield a higher rate than you can get at home.

As an example, the top 1-year certificate of deposit rates in the US currently return around 0.9% whereas Chinese deposits give out over 2.5%. And as China has a fiscally sound economy, the chance of losing your money there is small. Furthermore, the currency of China, (the Remnimbi), is widely seen as being grossly undervalued due to government controls. Once the currency becomes open to trade it is likely to appreciate, which means hot money investments will be worth more.

As stated, hot money should be welcomed by a recipient country since it can fuel economic growth and lead to higher standards of living overall. There are also benefits for developed countries investing overseas, since investors can achieve better diversification for their portfolios.

Problems arise when money flows in for just a short period. It leads to the growth of asset bubbles and short-term inflation that can then burst when the money flows are reversed. Hot money flows were one of the main causes attributed to the 1997 East Asian financial crisis that began when Thailand attempted to float its currency (the Thai Baht).

Thailand had built up a huge amount of debt at the time and was effectively bankrupt. However, as speculators began to pull money out of their overseas investments, it caused ripple effects that saw many traders reverse their hot money positions. This led to a big pullout of foreign money causing several Asian currencies to fall in value and Asian asset values to crash.

Although the negative and positive sides of hot money can be seen, it is equally true that such flows are essentially the results of central bank manipulations that lead to inequalities within global markets. In a completely free market, the incentives for making such flows would likely not exist.

HOW TO SPOT A CURRENCY CRISIS

Since the advent of paper money, there have been numerous examples of currency crises which have caught many investors off guard. In fact, some of the most dramatic examples have been in relatively recent times.

In 1994, for example, the Mexican peso crumbled, leaving it massively devalued and resulting in the country needing financial aid from the United States. Although there were many factors that caused the peso to crash, ultimately it was the result of a contraction in Mexican economic growth and the emptying of the country's foreign reserves. As the government overextended itself, traders feared the country would default on its debt. There were warning signs at the time and Mexico's current account deficit stood at 7% of GDP.

Then, in 1997, a similarly painful currency crisis occurred in Asia as many of the 'tiger' economies experienced a rapid withdrawal of 'hot money' and foreign investment. Like the peso, many of the Asian economies were supported by large amounts of foreign debt and when this was taken away there was the fear that large current account deficits for those countries would lead to government default; particularly among countries whose currencies were kept fixed.

Warning signs

To understand why a country may experience a currency crisis is no more difficult than looking at your own personal finance situation. If you have borrowed beyond your means, maxed out your credit cards and have less coming in than going out, you are in financial peril.

In the same way, a country which relies too heavily on borrowed funds always faces the risk of being unable to pay off its debts. If something bad happens, such as a negative economic shock or a crisis in sentiment, that risk can be intensified and the nation's currency is likely to suffer.

Deficits

One of the biggest warning signs of a full-blown crisis can be found in the current accounts of particular nations. A current account deficit essentially means that a country is spending more than it is receiving and economists generally regard current account deficits greater than 5 (as a percentage of GDP) to be unsustainable.

Uncertainty

As well as negative current account deficits, political instability and market sentiment can be a big driver when currencies are in danger. In 1994, for example, the stability of the Mexican peso was thrown into further turmoil by the assassination of a presidential candidate.

Anything that causes uncertainty is likely to lead to investors pulling their money out of a currency quickly and this leads to a rapid depreciation in its value.

Overvalued

Another factor that can ultimately push a currency over the edge is if it has been significantly bought up in the first place. Currency moves typically take a long time to play out so that economies are better able to adjust to new pressures.

However, if a country's exchange rate rises rapidly, those pressures may become exaggerated. Central banks try to adjust to the new environment quickly and may well do too much. The result is that the same speculators that bid the currency up in the first place are likely to bid it down just as quickly.

USING THE MARTINGALE TECHNIQUE

The martingale strategy is a money management technique that became popular in the 18th century by proposing the unlikely possibility of a 100% profitable betting strategy. Invented by French mathematician, Paul Pierre Levy, the idea behind the martingale technique is simple enough. It involves 'doubling down' whenever a losing bet is encountered. This way, the next winning bet is guaranteed to win back all the money lost, plus a little bit more.

Unfortunately, many studies have shown that the martingale strategy is fundamentally flawed since it requires the gambler to have infinite wealth.

Roulette

To see this in action, imagine a roulette player who always bets on red. The player's first bet of $1 loses so he doubles down and places another bet of $2. That loses again, so he places a bet of $4. Finally, the player wins and receives back $8, thereby making a $1 profit, since he has spent $7 and now has $8.

The problem is that the chances of each spin landing on red or black are the same each time. That means that a long run of blacks would mean the roulette player could quite easily run out of money. After eight blacks in a row, the player would need to bet $256 in order to win back his money.

You may think that eight blacks in a row is unlikely, but it does happen. And there is another problem too. Casinos know all about the martingale technique, which is why they introduce a table limit (often at the $200 level) and each table is assigned two green numbers (0 and 00). By doing so, they destroy the 50-50 probability of the bet, meaning any money management strategy for roulette is doomed to have a negative expectancy.

Trading

In trading, the martingale approach is equally as risky. Here, instead of there being two green numbers like on a roulette wheel, traders must pay commissions by means of a spread. Furthermore, although there is no limit to trade size, trends can go on for much longer than on a roulette table, which means the martingale strategy can run into trouble even quicker.

To trade with the martingale strategy requires the markets to be perfectly mean reverting (like a 50-50 coin toss) but we know that they are not. Financial markets can go in the same direction for very long periods.

Adding to losers

Using the martingale approach in trading, therefore, requires averaging down so that you are continually adding to your losers. If you buy the EUR/USD at 1.36, for example, and it falls to 1.35, you have to double your stake and go long again. If it goes down to 1.34, the same theory applies. By using this technique you can rack up your losses extremely quickly. And when you finally use up all your capital, you face a margin call and will be wiped out in just one trade

HOW TO CHOOSE THE BEST FOREX BROKER

The forex market is a $2 trillion industry, so it comes as a surprise to some, that instead of having one central exchange like the stock market, forex prices are maintained by the big market players (the banks) who deal and trade with each other via the 'interbank' market. However, to trade the interbank market is not possible for the majority of ordinary traders, since to do so would require a vast amount of money and credit with the banks.

Retail forex brokers solve this problem by acting as the middle man between the bank and the trader, but as with anything, some brokers are better than others.

Some brokers offer barely competitive prices, some brokers take the other side of your trades and some brokers may even manipulate spreads.

Regulation

The first question to ask when selecting a forex broker is whether they are regulated by a professional body. If not, it could be a sign that the broker is not up to scratch in one or more areas of its business. There are many regulating bodies around the world who work to make sure that brokers are secure and dependable. The main ones in the US are the National Futures Association and the Commodities Futures Trading Commission. There are also separate bodies for the UK, Australia, Germany and many more. This information can normally be found in the 'About' section of a broker's website.

Spreads

These days, most retail brokers earn money not off commissions or trading fees, but the spread with which they offer each market. Essentially, a broker makes money by buying the interbank rate and then selling a slightly wider rate to its customers. There is nothing wrong nor illegal with this, but it means retail brokers are essentially market makers. This is the reason why a trader might want to shop around to find the tightest spreads.

Furthermore, some brokers may take the other side of your trades or may advertise spreads that are tighter than they actually are. The best thing to do is to test the broker out for yourself using a demo account, to see whether the spreads are consistent with market rates.

Typically, ECN brokers, which have no dealing desk, tend to be closer to the interbank market and thereby offer tighter spreads. They are also thought to be more honest in terms of taking the other sides of trades and upholding true market prices.

Features

Forex brokers tend to come in all shapes and sizes. Some seem to come with just a trading platform and a few charts, whereas others offer up a whole host of advanced functionality and features. As a trader, you must decide what features you need to be able to trade effectively and what features you can do without. Does the trading platform respond quickly enough? Are different entries (such as limit orders) available? Is one-click trading enabled? Does the broker offer back-testing or MetaTrader compatibility? A broker does not need to have all the bells and whistles, but it does need to have enough functionality to enable you to feel comfortable in your trading setup.

There are other factors that are important when selecting a broker too, such as the level of margin available or amount of leverage. Generally, the higher the level of margin available, the smaller the size of account that can be opened. ECN brokers meanwhile, tend to require the largest account minimums.

Support

Customer service is always a key concern when deciding on a forex

225

broker, since if you have a problem it is nice to know there is someone on the other side who is able to help you out. As a bare minimum, your broker should provide telephone support during market hours in case your machine crashes and you need to close an open position. As with any company, poor customer service often belies deficiencies in the business elsewhere, so it pays to search out a broker that puts its customers at the top of its priorities.

Reputation

The beauty of the Internet is that information is more freely available than ever before, which is why one of the best ways to choose a forex broker is to simply look around to see what other people say about them. Online forums and message boards provide great places to find unbiased opinions from people who have used the services of a particular broker and can attest to their reliability. Similarly, industry magazines often provide independent reviews of brokers and also list those brokers who have managed to win awards for their services.

Other than message boards and magazines, a lot can be gained just by looking over a website. Does the website contain a lot of marketing and sales information or does it present itself in a professional way with the customer's interests at heart? Also, is the broker a big, established player in the market and does it offer up much in the way of guidance and educational materials to new traders?

Another thing to consider is what a broker does with your funds while they are not being used. Some brokers may pay you a small amount of interest for keeping it there while others may charge. Likewise, some brokers go to lengths to secure your capital in a bond, which protects it in the event of bankruptcy.

Conclusion

As you can see, there is a lot to think about when selecting a forex broker. The information may seem overwhelming but it's important to do your due diligence since you are essentially putting real money at risk. Most brokers offer free demonstrations as a way to try out their trading platforms risk free. Demos are generally the best way of getting to know a new broker. Together with advice from blogs and the investment community, it should not be too hard to find the broker right for you.

WHAT IS A FOREX EXPERT ADVISOR?

A forex expert advisor is a trading idea or strategy that has been written in MQL-4 programming language for the MetaTrader 4 trading platform. It can be a completely mechanical trading system that enters trades into a live market or it can be used to back-test data and flag signals for a trader to process manually.

Expert advisors are able to communicate directly to the broker via the MetaTrader platform and can manage all aspects of the trading process such as entering positions, managing risk and adjusting stops. By doing so, forex expert advisors take the emotion out of trading and, thereby, enable a trader to make profits without getting caught up in the stress and confusion of trading with a discretionary approach.

Since forex expert advisors are made up of sophisticated algorithms, they are also able to trade with a higher degree of accuracy and speed than a human trader. And due to the flexibility of the MQL-4 programming language, almost any indicator – strategy or trading idea – can be easily translated into code and then put into action.

Types of expert advisors

Coding an expert advisor (EA) in MQL-4 means there almost limitless possibilities for testing out different trading strategies. Some of the most common strategies are illustrated here:

Scalper EA

Scalping strategies aim to pick up small profits in markets from very quick trades and usually have no bias in market direction. They exist to exploit short-term inefficiencies in markets and are essentially one up from high frequency trading. Scalping strategies lend themselves very well to EAs since they rely on very fast executions that are often better made by a robot than a human trader. Whereas human scalpers can be prone to errors, scalper EAs can execute trades with 100% accuracy and as fast as is the connection between broker and server.

Breakout EA

Just as they are with discretionary traders, breakouts are popular strategies amongst EAs. EAs programmed to trade on a breakout often use technical indicators such as Bollinger Bands, ATR or price action levels. They take all the stress out of manual trading and allow the trader to sit back and watch the EA do the work.

News EA

Trading the news can be difficult for a manual trader, since it often requires lightning fast reactions and a strong stomach. Some expert advisors, however, are designed to trade news releases. They can be set up to trade only at certain times of day and thrive on the volatility created by news and economic announcements.

Hedging EA

Forex markets are ideal for hedging strategies and allow traders to buy one currency pair and sell another with the hope of profiting from one or both pairs. The ability to hedge trades accurately is often difficult for the human trader though, because risk needs to be constantly calculated versus position size and exposure to the market. Thankfully, hedging EAs can make these calculations in a split second, so are perfect for running these types of strategies.

Trend following EA

Essentially, EAs can be designed to work on any idea or strategy.

Many EAs are based on trend following and enter positions at the beginning of a trend and stay with it until a pre-determined profit target is hit or the logic of the system causes the EA to exit. They can be designed for different time frames too.

Advantages of using expert advisors

As already noted, EAs take the emotion out of trading. This means, instead of forex trading being a wild rollercoaster ride of missed profits – fear, greed and stress – trading becomes disciplined, professional and stress-free. EAs are able to do the calculations needed to run any type of forex strategy and can run them while you're asleep. This brings a huge benefit to traders, as it means you no longer have to sit in front of a computer all day staring at your screen. Expert advisors take all the hard work and stress out of trading. All the hard work is done before you trade – in developing and testing trading ideas.

Execution speeds are clearly another advantage associated with EAs. Many times, a robot performs complex trading maneuvers and does so in a blink of an eye. However, expert advisors offer more than simply speed and the minimization of emotional trading.

EAs are indispensable since they provide an objective analysis of any trading idea. Traders often come up with trading ideas and strategies, but due to the limits of the human brain, it is impossible to know whether that strategy would have stood up over past data. Expert advisors can eliminate this doubt by proving (with statistical confidence) how profitable a strategy really is. They can be tested and optimized over several years of historical data and it usually only takes a few minutes. Of course, the end result is that an EA is capable of saving (or earning) a trader thousands of dollars in the long run.

How to use a forex expert advisor

The first step to using an expert advisor is to download the Meta-Trader4 platform. EAs can then be installed to the 'Experts' folder.

MetaTrader actually ships with several free built-in EAs for you to try out in your own time.

There are also many EAs available for sale on the Internet, some of which are very profitable and easy to use while some are terrible. For many EA products, there is no need to know how to code. All the information for installing and using the bot is included with purchase and usually only takes a few minutes to get going.

If you want to develop your own EAs you need to learn how to code, (unless you want to pay a programmer to do the work for you). If you are not a programmer, probably the best thing to do would be to learn C programming since MQL-4 and C are extremely similar. Once you have knowledge of how to code, you can code your own indicators and systems and have access to a whole new world of forex trading.

10 TIPS AND TRICKS FOR USING METATRADER 4

When it comes to choosing a trading platform, MetaTrader 4 can be pretty much do it all. It's got good charts, loads of indicators, has automated trading functionality and even allows the testing of trading systems and EAs.

However, with so many features on offer it can sometimes get a bit confusing for beginners. So here are 10 tips designed to help!

1. Keyboard shortcuts

There are plenty of keyboard shortcuts available for MetaTrader 4 that speed things up no end. Here are the most useful ones:

Arrow keys	Use to scroll through the chart window
Home	Moves the chart to the first bar
End	Moves the chart to the current bar

Backspace	Deletes most recent drawing
F4	Opens MetaEditor
F9	Opens 'New Order' window
F10	Opens 'Pop-up Prices' window
F11	Enables full screen mode
Alt + 2	Displays candlesticks charts
Ctrl + A	Arranges all indicator window heights by default
Ctrl + N	Opens 'Navigator' window

2. How to add an EA

To add a custom made indicator or EA to the platform, first copy the source code and activate the MetaEditor by pressing F4. Then, open the expert advisor wizard and click the relevant field, custom indicator or EA. Click next, give the indicator or EA a name and then click 'Finish'. Finally, click your left mouse button in the screen window, select the whole code and then paste it. Save it by pressing F5.

3. How to set up a template

Templates are useful for those times when you have set up a chart with all your favorite settings but then end up making a mess of it and don't know how to get it back. Often, instead of working out how to reverse the changes, it can be simpler to load up a saved version of the chart itself, as it was before. This can be done by saving a template of your chart first. Simply open up a chart then press F8 to open settings and save the chart in the templates menu with a memorable name. Now you can reload the template at any time from the charts menu.

4. How to save a profile

Just like a template saves the layout of a chart, it is also possible to save groups of charts and windows so that your screen layout stays the same whenever you open the program. By clicking on the 'Profiles' icon and selecting 'Save Profile As', you can save the current layout as it appears on the screen. This way, you can save lots of different profile layouts for individual users. Simply re-select a profile by going to the 'Profiles' icon again and selecting from the drop down menu.

5. How to add to favorites

If you have a certain number of indicators, EAs or scripts that you constantly use and need easy access to, you can set them up as favorites and call them up whenever needed. Simply hover over the indicator or script you want to add with your mouse, right click and then choose 'Add to Favorites'.

6. How to add trend lines to a chart

Trend lines are often used by traders to show the current direction of the trend and to indicate areas of support and resistance in markets. To add a trend line in MetaTrader 4, click the 'Trendline' icon then click and drag with the mouse. To make changes, double click on the area where the trend line is.

If you hold down the CTRL key while drawing the trend line, it makes it perfectly parallel. If you right click on the line, you can make changes to the color, style and other parameters.

7. How to use crosshair mode and the ruler tool

The ruler tool in MetaTrader 4 can be useful for calculating the number of pips between two points in a chart (such as if you want to measure how many pips away your stop loss is to your current trade). To access the ruler, first switch to crosshair mode by pressing CTRL+F keys. In crosshair mode, you can now see all the price, date and time coordinates at any point on the chart.

Now, simply click the chart at the point where you want to measure from and, holding down the left mouse key, drag to where you want to complete the measurement. The ruler appears and forms a line showing how many bars to the right or left of the cursor, the pip count and the price at the point of the cursor.

8. How to see your account history

Sometimes it is useful to see your account history, although this is usually best done at the end of the day so as not to disturb your trading. To see details of all your trades, go to the 'Terminal' panel and select 'Account History'. You can then click on any of the positions you are interested in and by dragging it into the main chart window, you are able to analyze the entry, target, exit, market data and other points of interest.

9. How to access the MQL4 community

The MQL4 community is a place where newbies and experienced programmers alike come together to answer each other's coding questions. It is a great place to find free support for any of your programming problems. As well as a forum, the community contains a website, book and code base – where examples of MQL4 code are frequently posted for traders to use free of charge. The community can be accessed via the MetaTrader 4 platform by clicking onto 'Tools' then 'MetaQuotes Language Editor' (or simply hit F4). Navigate to 'Help' and click on the MQL4 Community drop down.

10. How to remove the live news feed

Although useful, some features of MetaTrader 4 can sometimes slow the software down. Features like the live news feed are especially bad for this but can be easily removed by following one simple step. Simply navigate to the 'Tools' menu, click 'Options' and then uncheck the box that says 'Enable News'. This should help speed things up. If not, you could also consider turning off the symbols that you never trade, for example SEKNOK.

REVIEW OF ZULUTRADE

ZuluTrade has a monthly trading turnover of around $3bn. The company is based out of Greece and is registered with both the NFA and CFTC.

Unlike some brokers, ZuluTrade does not hold any money or execute trades. Instead, ZuluTrade connects your chosen trading strategies directly with your broker.

To get started on ZuluTrade is simple. A quick form from your broker authorizes ZuluTrade to act on your behalf and then once you login to the platform you can begin selecting the kind of systems you are interested in.

The ZuluTrade concept

The whole point of ZuluTrade is to be able to mimic exactly the trades of your chosen 'experts' and once registered this is easy to do.

The first thing to do is to login where you will be able to search from over 77,000 'expert' traders. Each one has their own unique strategy and risk profile and is listed with certain criteria such as drawdown information, ROI and their equity chart. From here, it's also easy to see the top 10 performing experts and the amount of money that is following each one. You can also sort them by their recent return.

Once you have found an expert you like the look of you can then instruct ZuluTrade to follow their trades. By being connected to the back end of your broker, ZuluTrade can then place the same trades as the expert automatically on your own account saving you the trouble of having to watch the screen.

Tips for using ZuluTrade

With so many experts to choose from, part of the key to success with ZuluTrade relies on being able to pick the right ones to follow.

It is therefore vital to pick experts that have robust trading strategies and not ones that have simply got lucky.

In this way, it is wise to study the equity curves of different experts and check their money management systems. An equity curve that is all over the place might be an unstable system while an equity curve that is too smooth, could be using an unsustainable technique such as the Martingale system.

The Martingale system works by continually doubling risk in order to win back losses but it will eventually end in ruin so always steer clear of these systems.

The best idea is to pick a number of carefully selected experts that are in line with your risk preferences but also offer realistic results. Experts that are doing unbelievably well are more likely to stop performing. You can then combine them in a basket of experts and see how well they perform

ABOUT THE AUTHOR

Joe B Marwood is an independent analyst and trader with more than five years' experience in financial markets. On September 16, just one day after Lehman Brothers filed for bankruptcy and the markets imploded, he began his career trading futures for an independent trading firm based in the city of London, England.

Although those first few months were tough, Marwood came out of the financial crisis largely unscathed and managed to make a number of timely calls in the markets, including correctly predicting the bottom in stocks in March 2009 by a couple of weeks, the flash crash top in 2011 by one week and the top in silver in 2011 by one day. He now runs his own private investment fund.

GLOSSARY OF TERMS

API

Application programming interface; an application that allows the backend connection of trading platforms and brokers.

Ask price

The best price a seller or broker accepts to sell a security.

Balance of trade

The difference between a country's imports and exports over a period of time, leading to a trade surplus or trade deficit.

Basis point

A unit that is 1/100 of 1%; mainly used to represent small changes in interest rates and bond yields.

Bearish

The belief that an investment will fall in price or that the market is in a bear market.

Bear market

A market that is generally considered to be falling in value. Officially, a bear market is a market that has gone down 20% or more over a period of at least 2 months.

Bid price

The best price a buyer or broker is willing to pay for a security.

Black box

Term for a trading system where the exact formulas or calculations are not necessarily seen or known.

Bottom up

Analysis that seeks to find undervalued companies by analyzing financial statistics relating to those individual companies rather than the sector or economy as a whole.

Bullish

The belief that an investment will rise in price or that the market is in a bull market.

Bull market

A market that is generally considered to be rising in value. Officially, a bull market is any market that has gone up 20% or more over a period of at least 2 months.

CD

Certificate of deposit; an investment which has a set interest rate to be paid throughout the duration of the investment.

CFD

Contract for difference; allows the trading of financial futures without the need to worry about the delivery of physical goods. Settled through cash payments.

CPI

Consumer price index; a measure of inflation within an economy using a basket of prices of various consumer goods.

Curve-fit

A system that is curve-fit is too closely optimized with past data and will not necessarily work in the future.

Default

The inability to pay one's financial obligations resulting in unintended consequences.

Depression

A severe downturn in economic activity, more prolonged than a recession.

Dovish

An outlook or statement that supports lower interest rates. Opposite to Hawkish.

Drawdown

The peak-to-trough decline of a portfolio or trading system. For example, a portfolio that has fallen 20% is in a 20% drawdown. See also, maximum drawdown.

EOD

Refers to end-of-day data; includes only the daily open, high, low and close values of a security. Unsuitable for short-term trading but can be used for testing daily or weekly trading systems.

Equity curve

Equity is how much capital it available at a point in time, taking into account open positions. The equity curve describes how the equity has performed over time.

ETF

Exchange traded fund; a security that tracks a basket or index of other securities and can be traded with the same characteristics as a stock.

Filter

A means of restricting the number or direction of trading opportunities.

Fundamental data

Quantitative data that relates to economic conditions such as GDP, unemployment or money supply.

GDP

Gross domestic product; the complete market value output of all official goods and services produced by a country.

Hawkish

An outlook or statement that supports higher interest rates. Opposite to dovish.

Hedge

An investment that is used to offset potential gains or losses on another investment.

Lag

The inherent delay that occurs when using indicators that are based on past data

Leverage

The use of financial assets or margin to increase potential returns on an investment. Also increases potential losses. See also, maximum leverage.

Liquidity

How easily a security can be bought or sold in the market without affecting the asset's price. Large numbers of buyers and sellers provide liquidity in a market meaning it is easier for traders to buy or sell an investment at a fair and efficient price.

Long

'Going long' means buying an investment in the belief that it will go up in value.

Lot

The standardized quantity of a financial instrument, futures traders typically trade in lots. The minimum number of lots available in a futures contract is 1 which usually equals $10 per pip.

Margin

Money that is borrowed to purchase securities and used to amplify returns, also amplifies losses.

Margin call

When securities bought on margin fall in value beyond a certain point, a broker demands an investor puts up additional money or sells assets in order to bring their account up to the account minimum.

Martingale

An unsustainable money management technique that involves increasing bet size after a loss in order to win back what was just lost. Martingale works for a time but will ultimately fail as it requires an unlimited supply of money.

Maturity

The period of time an investment such as a bond remains outstanding. Once a bond matures, the principal must be repaid to the bondholder with interest or face default.

Maximum drawdown

The maximum peak-to-trough decline that a system or portfolio is expected to face. This number is drawn from historical testing. A trading system that falls more than the maximum drawdown in testing means that it could be broken.

Maximum leverage

The maximum size of a trade permitted in a leveraged account. At maximum leverage, just a small price movement could wipe out an entire account.

Monte Carlo method

Running many simulations of a trading system in order to calculate the probabilities of various outcomes.

Noise

Short-term movements in an investment that has no underlying reason and is not thought to bear little significance to the future movement of that security.

Overshoot

When a signal exceeds its target resulting in inaccurate representation of the price

Pip

Similar to a tick, a pip is the smallest increment by which a currency quote can change. For example, 'EURUSD went up 20 pips to 1.3280'.

Point

Similar to a tick or pip but usually denoting larger price moves. For example, 'the Dow Jones is 200 points away from its all-time high'.

QE

Quantitative easing; the purchase of assets in order to induce liquidity and spur economic growth instigated as part of central bank monetary policy.

Rally

The term rally is used to signify a market that is going higher in price.

Random walk

The belief that markets are efficient at processing information and thus the price movement of securities is not predictable.

Range

The difference between the high and low price of a security.

Recession

A period of economic decline usually indicated by a fall in GDP over 2 or more consecutive quarters.

Round trip or round turn

The full cost associated with opening and closing a trade including the bid and ask spread and any additional commissions or taxes.

Short

'Going short' means selling an investment in the belief that it will go down and you can buy it back at a lower price for a profit.

Small cap/large cap

Denotes markets' capitalization of a stock, in effect how much the company is worth at current prices. Companies worth between $300m and $2bn are generally considered small caps while large caps are typically worth $10bn or over.

Spike

When a market moves violently in one direction within a short space of time.

Spread

The difference between the bid and ask price of a security or the cost of making a trade.

T-Bill

Treasury bill; a short-term, 'ultra-safe' debt obligation backed by the US government with a maturity of less than 1 year.

Tick

Synonymous with pip, a tick is the minimum upward or downward movement of a security. Normally used in the stock market. For example, 'the Dow Jones went up 20 ticks today'.

Top down

Analysis that seeks to find profitable investments by looking at big picture macro-economic factors and trends and then breaking those components down into more detail.

US retail sales

Monthly report released by the Census Bureau and Department of Commerce detailing an aggregated measure of sales in retail goods in the previous month.

Walk-forward analysis

The repeated testing of a system on out-of-sample and in-sample data, shifting forward through time periods.

Whipsaw

Occurs when a market moves in one direction giving the impression a strong trend is in place, before reversing sharply the other way. A constant source of frustration for trend traders.

Yield

Synonymous with return; a bond yielding 3% per annum returns 3% a year.

Index

Symbols

1987 crash 22, 43

A

Adaptive moving average 161
ADX indicator 154
American Depository Receipts 92
Animal spirits 35
API 237
ATR 165, 166, 167, 198, 228
Average true range 165

B

Back-test 114
Balance sheet 59, 62
Bank of China 32
Bank of Japan 33
Barrons 64
Benjamin Graham 61
Bernanke 30, 31, 50, 97
Big trends 20, 25, 27, 67, 72
Bilateral triangles 129
Black marubozu 136
Black Wednesday 25
BOE 32
Boiler room 213
Bollinger bands 139
Bonds 45, 91, 93, 96, 97, 106, 110
Breaking the buck 43
Breakouts 128, 142
Bruce Kovner 121
Bullish and bearish engulfing 138

C

Candlesticks 135
CAR 177
Carry trade 217, 218
Central banks 29
  Bank of England 25, 29, 32, 210
  European Central Bank 29, 31, 210
  Federal Reserve 29, 30, 31, 51, 210
Charles H. Dow 63
China 93, 106, 107, 219
Chris Camillo 90

Commercial traders 65
Commissions 110, 113, 179, 213, 223, 224, 242
Commitment of Traders Report 65
Compounding 94, 95, 179
Conference calls 88
CPI 97
Crossover 146, 153
Currency prices 47
Current account balance 47, 48, 49
Current ratio 58
Curve-fit 174, 175, 177, 238
Cyclical stocks 38

D

Day trade 130
Day traders 22
DCA 73, 74, 186
Debt to equity 58
Deflation 37
Delisted stocks 179
Directional movement index 152
Diversification 81, 90, 110
DMI 152
Doji 136
Dollar cost averaging 73, 186
Double bottom 129
Double top 128
Dow Jones industrial average 56
Dow Theory 63, 206
Dr. Alexander Elder 121
Dr Howard Bandy 176

E

Earnings per share 57
ECB 32
Ed Seykota 120
Equity curve 177, 178, 184, 191, 235, 239
Euphoria 84
Exotic investments 90
Expert advisor 227, 229, 231
Exponential moving average 160
Extreme point rule 153

F

Facebook 89, 104, 207

.

Made in the USA
Lexington, KY
16 November 2014